A DIALOGUE OF LIFE

A DIALOGUE OF LIFE

TOWARDS THE ENCOUNTER
OF JEWS AND CHRISTIANS

Silvina Chemen & Francisco Canzani

New City Press
of the Focolare
Hyde Park, NY

JTS

The Jewish
Theological
Seminary
New York, NY

Published in the United States by

New City Press
202 Comforter Blvd., Hyde Park, NY 12538
www.newcitypress.com

and

The Jewish Theological Seminary
3080 Broadway, New York, NY 10027
www.jtsa.edu

Original title published in Spanish
Un diálogo para la vida : hacia el encuentro entre judíos y
cristianos: a dos voces y al unísono
© Ciudad Nueva, Buenos Aires: 2013 (ISBN 978-950-586-298-6)

Cover design by Leandro de Leon and Andrew Re

Translated by Carlos Bajo

Library of Congress Cataloging-in-Publication Data

Chemen, Silvina, author.
 [Dialogo para la vida. English]
 A dialogue of life : towards the encounter of Jews and Christians / by
Silvina Chemen & Francisco Canzani.
  pages cm
 "Original title published in Spanish: Un dialogo para la vida."
 Summary: "This book written by a Rabbi and a Christian outlines the
challenges and opportunities of genuine interreligious dialogue. It shows
that it is possible to educate in the art of dialogue without losing our
identity. It requires the commitment to listening, which implies also
knowing how to be silent"-- Provided by publisher.
 ISBN 978-1-56548-562-4 (alk. paper)
 1. Judaism--Relations--Christianity. 2. Christianity and other
religions--Judaism. 3. Dialogue--Religious aspects. I. Canzani, Francisco,
author. II. Title.
 BM535.C511513 2015
 261.2'6--dc23
                              2015003213

Printed in the United States of America

Contents

Acknowledgments

THE WORD "GRATITUDE" COMES from the Latin word *gratus*, which means pleasing, agreeable, grateful.

It gives us joy to express our gratitude because this book was made possible by a countless number of people and life situations that allowed us to be who we are and to say what we think and do.

We wish to thank:

our families, who accompanied us with so much love throughout the writing of the text;

our communities: the Community Bet El and the Focolare Movement, for their trust and for being spaces of realization of the ideals of dialogue;

Chiara Lubich, for her inspiration and for having opened up spaces of encounter between Jews and Christians;

Rabbi Daniel Goldman, master of the dialogical encounter, for his text in the Appendix, and for his fraternal support;

the members of the Center for Interreligious Dialogue of the Focolare Movement: Roberto Catalano, Christina Lee, Joseph Sievers, Miriam Girardi, Paul Lemarie, for their support, their contributions to the editing and their shared life experiences;

Bishop Ramón Dus and Rabbi Jack Bemporad, true pillars of our shared journey, for their generous endorsements;

Beppe Milan, Daniel Martínez, Cristina Calvo, Osvaldo De Piero and Francesco Ballarini, for their generosity in sharing ideas and texts;

Eduardo Zaffaroni and Silvia Kobryniec, our first readers; a Christian and a Jew who first approached the text with dedication and responsibility and gave us invaluable feedback;

Maria Teresa D'Auria and Sonia Vargas, for their suggestions;

Héctor Shalom, for his meticulous and loving reading of the book and his support and companionship in life;

Ilán and Ariel, youth of dialogue and companions in life;

Damián García, editor of this book, for his friendship, motivation and constant support during the process of our work;

Lorena Klappenbach, our proofreader, for her valuable suggestions and her personal closeness;

our fellows in dialogue in Buenos Aires: Marvi Yofre, Graciela Maggio, Jorge and Patricia Callejo;

the power of the dreams and the encouragement of Russ Peárce, Renata Dias, Rabbi Tsvi Blanchard;

Rabbi Burton Visotzky, for his empowerment and the responsibility and love for the English edition;

The Jewish Theological Seminary for their support in making the English edition possible;

the editorial team at New City Press, especially Jim Webber, for their profound and committed work;

Carlos Bajo, for his respectful translation and Tom Hartman for his patient and thorough proofreading.

Prologues

I ACCEPTED THE INVITATION MADE by Silvina Chemen and Francisco Canzani to write a few lines to introduce this book because I feel I am part of the project and the experience that you will discover in these pages. It is a project called dialogue, a word that is on everyone's lips in our times. Nonetheless, dialogue is still an almost unknown or poorly understood concept, especially in its vital aspect. In fact, dialogue should be "lived." It is not a concept to philosophize about, particularly when it has not been experienced.

Dialogue is an experience that becomes lifestyle, language, a way of looking at the other and the world. Paul VI, true prophet of dialogue and central figure in the post-Vatican II opening of the Catholic Church to other creeds and cultures, always said that the world today needs more witnesses than teachers, and he decided to listen to the latter, if they were also witnesses. The authors of this text, which aims to be a training tool for the formation in dialogue, are masters of dialogue and formation, and this book is the fruit of their careful work. However, first and foremost, Chemen and Canzani bear witness that dialogue is possible.

In fact, these pages were born from the following experience, as written to me by Rabbi Silvina Chemen: "Francisco and I tried to craft a text that developed step by step during our conversations, our meetings and even through our e-mails. It is a book which bears the traces of many others, and which was enriched by the experiences and the lessons that we learned from people in different situations. Above all, the experience of writing together was so deep and spiritual that we felt the presence of the Divine between us, with us and in us."

Dialogue is a journey and the authors help us travel along it. They begin with a reflection about the ultimate existential question: "Who am I?" and they eventually end with dreams open to the future. We cannot commit to dialogue without dreaming. Through these pages we can see that dialogue is a demand and a response for people, a relationship in which people try to give of themselves and get to know each other, just as they are.

This book was born from the mutual gift and knowledge among the authors, although not exclusively. It contains pages that, as we read them, allow us "to do the experience of the other," as Martin Buber would say.

Beneath the ideas that are presented here, we can find a certainty: dialogue is possible today, also between Christians and Jews or between anyone with whom it might seem impossible to dialogue with. The experience of the authors, the very origin of this book, allows us to state that it is possible to educate in the art of dialogue without losing our own identity. On the contrary, we will find it again more solid than what it was before.

Undoubtedly, there is a necessary, crucial condition to do all this, which the book develops exhaustively: the commitment to listening, which implies also knowing how to be silent, to make silence. Silence constitutes a key element in the encounter with whoever comes from a different culture or from a religion different from ours. Silence forces us to leave aside the rush and the frenzy of the globalized world that pulls us with it every day. Silence is not just being quiet, it is creating inside of us a space for the other.

Ancient Greeks used a particularly meaningful word to indicate the effort made by tragic actors in order to penetrate the daily lives of men and women: "empathy." Empathy, in its original root, means to feel in oneself, that is, to put oneself totally in the others' shoes, up to the point in which I can feel as mine their sufferings and joys, in order to understand and help them effectively. It implies trying to see the world as the other does. It requires, obviously, the ability of forgetting about myself so that the others can tell me who they are and can offer to me their "difference." The great Raimon Panikkar affirmed how important it is "to understand my neighbor as he understands himself."[1] This is the reason why, as we are constantly and beautifully reminded by the pages of this book, listening becomes an indispensable condition.

A few years ago, during a Jewish-Christian congress, I was struck by what an American rabbi said. He affirmed with conviction: "it's not a matter of convincing the other or agreeing with everything he says. It is, rather, accepting that it is possible to think differently from the way I think. It's a question of believing in the possibility of the other."[2]

Dialogue holds an immense value and promotes fraternity. Chiara Lubich had discovered this during the Second World War, when she was a young Italian teacher. As founder of the Focolare Movement, during the following decades, she opened new roads for dialogue between men and women of different cultures and religions all over the world. Even if it might have seemed foolish at the time, just a few years after the world was at war, she proposed this to a group of friends: "Before all else, the soul must always fix its gaze on the one Father of many children, Then, it must see all as children of the same Father. In mind and in heart we must always go beyond the bounds imposed on us by human life alone and create the habit of constantly opening ourselves to the reality of being one human family in one Father: God."[3] This involved a change of perspective, a different way of looking at the other: "The person next to me was created as a gift for me and I was created as a gift for the person next to me. On earth all stands in a relationship of love

---

1. Panikkar, R., *The Intrareligious Dialogue*, New York: Paulist Press, 1978, p. 12.
2. Cf. Editorial, *Gen's Magazine*, XV (2007) 3, pp. 1–4, published by Focolare Movement in Mumbai, India.
3. Lubich, Chiara, *The Art of Loving*, New York: New City Press, 2010, p. 31.

with all: each thing with each thing."[4] Lubich's perspective and her proposal of dialogue play an important part in these pages, becoming an educational methodology.

At this time of history, in the midst of globalization, migration flows, threats of conflicts among groups and communities, unexpected outbreaks of anti-Semitism, but also of the opening of many opportunities that humanity did not have before, each of us is called to be a creator of encounters, not just to avoid the clash of civilizations, but to give our own and indispensable contribution to a different world.

There is no doubt that this book can prepare us to have a leading role in this new springtime, and encourage us to involve everybody in this project of dialogue, which is at the same time a prophecy and a dream, our families, our groups and communities, everybody with whom we might be in contact with.

Roberto Catalano
Director
International Center for Interreligious Dialogue
Focolare Movement

4. Lubich, Chiara, *Essential Writings*, New York: New City Press, 2007, p. 87.

V ATICAN II, WITH ITS document *Nostra Aetate* (Our Age) was a revolutionary development in interreligious relations. For the first time, the Catholic Church sought to examine its relationships with other religions, and especially the Jewish Faith.

It addressed numerous concerns that the Jewish community had expressed with respect to past Catholic teachings of contempt. It courageously rejected the Jews' collective responsibility for deicide, it reaffirmed the position of the Apostle Paul that the gifts and promises that God made to Israel were irrevocable, and it began a process which, with later Vatican documents, tried to confront the issue of anti-Judaism and proper relations between Christians and Jews.

These documents, extraordinarily important, were available to scholars and Church officials, and those concerned with interreligious dialogue. However, it is of the utmost importance that this development should not be limited to academic discussions. It is important that Christians and Jews in synagogues, and churches, and in schools, be made aware of this in a way that is both honest and constructive.

What is unique in Silvina Chemen and Francisco Canzani's book is that they succeed better than any other book known to me in dealing with the challenges and the opportunities of genuine interreligious dialogue. Both authors are extraordinarily sensitive and wise; they offer ways in which our two communities can work together and learn from one another, and find a common basis for dealing with the ethical and political issues of our day. This book provides great insight and hopefully, it will be used as a basis for study, discussion, and action in our interreligious communities.

Rabbi Jack Bemporad
Director, Center for Interreligious Understanding,
New Jersey, U.S.A., and Professor and Director
John Paul II Center, Angelicum,
St. Thomas Aquinas University,
Rome, Italy

JEWISH-CHRISTIAN RELATIONS HAVE A long and often painful history. As a result, the pathway toward a more fraternal relationship may seem at times hard and rough. Both authors are well aware of these difficulties and they show ways toward dialogue that are not just theory or academic statements. Silvina Chemen and Francisco Canzani offer a journey that might appear too simple, but it requires the commitment of the whole person. They identify as an indispensable and fundamental element for dialogue the trust that must be given, received and built together. They stress the importance of listening before speaking. Their advice regarding how to ask questions and, especially how not to ask questions to the other, reveals a wisdom that comes from many years of experience. However, this is not just an optimistic book. It confronts many real problems that appear in the process of dialogue; it offers answers that come from life experiences and it never gets swamped before complicated situations.

I know many books about the relationship between Jews and Christians, some written by a Jew and by a Christian. This book is different, unique, I would say, because it is born after a long journey together. It offers the fruits of this journey and, with a careful pedagogy, opens ways to carry ahead a dialogue between Jews and Christians, and not just among them! It is respectful of identities and asymmetries, while being profound and fascinating. I wish many people could read it.

Joseph Sievers
Professor of Jewish History and Literature of the
Hellenistic Period
Pontifical Biblical Institute, Rome

Introduction

ACH OF US HAS been involved in the dialogue between Jews and Christians for years, from our own development and work. We have had many successes and failures in this process of trial and error that allow us to encounter each other with freedom and certainty. Ciudad Nueva Publishing House invited us to write about dialogue and specifically about the pedagogy of dialogue. The world speaks today about the need for dialogue among religions as a premise for true peace, especially in regions threatened by religious conflicts. Although the mass media covers interfaith topics with more or less depth, unfortunately they usually show only the conflicts among religions and the extremists present in them.

There is, however, little experience about interfaith dialogue. It has been left to religious leaders, scholars, and people with a special vocation to build bridges among different people. It has never been very popular and it has never become a major issue, even among the faithful of our own respective religions, Jewish and Christian.

Nevertheless right from the beginning, people committed to Jewish-Christian dialogue have tried to make this dialogue penetrate down to ordinary Jews and Christians. Wide sectors of our religious traditions are aware of the importance of dialogue. There are many valuable publications about this and testimonies of inspiring experiences of close relationships. We might have reached the time to conceptualize what individuals have learned and to transform them in to ways of thinking and teaching how one dares to share with the others such important moments of life.

We are not educators with graduate degrees but people with the "degree" of "learners and multipliers of dialogue" because we have taken the vital decision to plunge into the adventure of meeting the other. We are different; we come from different faith traditions; we have inherited a difficult history; and we recognize that prejudice and stigmas are present in many of our fellow believers. In spite of all that, we are full of hope, and it has grown since we began to write this book because of the number of expressions of encouragement and joy from many other people.

Is a pedagogy of dialogue necessary? Are we not dialogical beings since we first began to speak? Is the good intention of getting in contact with the other not sufficient? Experience has taught us that when we talk about religious beliefs, much is not expressed, there are sensitive topics to share, dark areas to discover and a lot to work on in our thought and expression. This is so because our intention is to generate something more than a formal and respectful encounter. We want to dream about a society in which—as Martin Buber said—people can confirm each other, because all of us desire to be confirmed by others in whom we are and who we can be.

In this book we try to "teach ourselves" to confirm the other, in all these dimensions; to get to know the other, to learn to listen, to learn how to ask those questions we never dared ask, to generate spaces of confidence, to climb over the obstacles that separate us. And do all this with sincerity and courage.

It is evident that dialogue is a matter of two, but in which each partner begins and takes the first step almost simultaneously. This is why we decided to call it *A Dialogue of Life*, because each of us speaks with his/her own voice, and yet this distinction does not deprive us of the possibility of meeting in a melody and to be able to sing in unison when the topics we discuss touch us in the same way. Each of us with our own voice and our own way of interpreting texts and realities. Each with the time to listen to the other, sometimes to answer, sometimes just receiving. Each with the peace of spirit given by the absence of the need to retort or defend because our words do not attack but are expressed with love and integrity. Every now and then we have been surprised by such an accord on some topics that we decided to write in unison because we were singing "the same song."

A Dialogue of Life: Towards the Encounter of Jews and Christians is designed to reach everybody. We want it to motivate Jews and Christians with any kind of involvement in their own religious communities, to begin the way of dialogue, to do something so valuable for human coexistence as building bridges between their religions, religions that share the same scriptures and the same territory but that know little of each other and have little relationship. These pages aim at providing accessible tools for anyone involved in encounters between people of different cultures or religions. We offer useful tools especially for those who work in the areas of education (catechists, teachers, professors) and for families, in order that we might create an environment to educate men and women capable of dialogue.

We share with you readers our experience of writing that goes beyond the work of publishing. We have been friends for several years and we have found ourselves working for a common goal in life: a world united in its diversity. As we advanced in our writing together, we confirmed this extraordinary experience: when the dialogue was sincere, deep and loving, we found ourselves in the divine presence. It went beyond our intellectual and rational capabilities. We found ourselves, over and over again, in a dimension that went beyond logic to give place to a full manifestation of the spirit. We have been absolutely happy in this work, and our greatest wish is to transmit to you this portion of "paradise" we have had the privilege of entering.

We have discussed everything together and we have corrected each other many times; we have been sensitive to and critical of each word and, at the same time, completely free to tell each other whatever was necessary so as to have this book rooted in reality and not just in the air of utopia. Throughout the process of writing we have experienced certain situations that have been included in the book with the intention of sharing with you that life itself is a great lesson for dialogue. The one thing necessary is to have an open heart and the will to improve and learn every day.

"In unison and in two voices" means more than just a report of a positive experience of dialogue from which some values can be drawn for those who were not personally involved. It uses different sources—from the Holy Scriptures to contemporary authors and Church documents—that deal with dialogue and constitute the theoretical framework which we employ in everyday life, in which our personal and community destinies are involved when we deal with interfaith dialogue.

It is a task that begins with life itself and tries to reach a reflection that can provide theoretical tools for action to advance in the initial experience. A kind of "virtuous circle" in which we want to be involved and involve many others.

We have learned so much that we included within the chapters a section called "learning on the way," in which we share the vicissitudes we faced in the process of writing, the decisions we made while we wrote, and what we learned in the process with the hope of sharing our ideas with you.

There are many pages still to be written because we see life as an opportunity for constant learning. We have faith in a more reciprocal and spacious humanity in which we can all feel that we have a place in the other's home.

We hope you enjoy this musical score full of hopes and beliefs.

Silvina and Francisco

Chapter 1

Starting Point — Why Dialogue?

In two separate voices: Silvina

Who am I?

I AM RABBI SILVINA CHEMEN, married to Héctor, and we have two children, Ariel and Ilán. Many years ago I decided that my vocation was to be a teacher and so my first career move was getting a degree to teach Hebrew and the Bible. Subsequently, at the University of Buenos Aires, I obtained a Bachelor's degree in Communication Sciences, and later on I pursued the Rabbinate at the Latin American Rabbinical Seminary of the Conservative Movement, where I received my rabbinic ordination. I began this road before finishing high school, actively participating in various roles within the community, taking on tasks of increasing responsibility in synagogues, congregations and Jewish schools. (It should be noted that since the Jewish tradition, unlike Christianity, has neither priests nor sacraments, qualified people can lead rituals and ceremonies in the synagogue.)

In the beginning I taught how to sing the liturgy. Later, I gave Bar-Bat Mitzvah lessons, preparing young people for entry into the adult liturgical community. I also taught Hebrew language and traditions, and the Bible in various schools, as well as Bible courses for adults. Eventually, I was appointed director of a Jewish school, becoming an assistant rabbi in several synagogues and finally a rabbi.

I come from a family of Arab origins, so we speak Arabic and eat Middle Eastern food in my house. This type of family was born into a culture where male authority was predominant. In addition, the image of the woman in the house was one of submission and respect. In this context it is quite unthinkable for a woman to reach a position similar to the one I have. However, in my family there have always been strong women who dared to leave the preset molds in order to dialogue with a broader and more inclusive world within the Jewish community.

In the sixties, Marshall T. Meyer,[1] an American rabbi, arrived in Argentina, and he brought a brand of religious training, within a current called "Conservative," which proposed equality of rights and responsibilities for men and women in the Jewish ritual, among other things. The arrival of this rabbi produced mixed reactions of devotion and staunch opposition.

I come from a family where women, starting with my great grandmother, fought for a place of equality, and thus they decided to adhere to this new trend. Rabbi Meyer used to say that one should enter the synagogue with the Torah (the Pentateuch) in one hand and the daily newspaper in the other.

For where there is a human being who suffers, the Jewish voice should appear in order to contribute to the dignity of the human condition; where there is someone who is hungry, there should be our money and our time to remove the scourge. Where Argentine citizens were stripped of the right to express themselves and be free, there Rabbi Marshall joined other defenders of the human condition, without distinction, to challenge and

1. Marshall T. Meyer (1930- 1993). Rabbi and teacher who arrived in Argentina from the United States in the late fifties and produced the largest religious revolution in Latin America, founding the Conservative Movement (the first movement of non-Orthodox Jews). He founded the Bet El community (to which I belong now as a rabbi) and the Latin American Rabbinical Seminary. A fierce human rights activist in the darkest days of Argentina, he was elected to be part of the CONADEP (National Commission on the Disappearance of Persons).

defend the human rights of all who lived in this land, risking even his own life.

God's plan has brought me today to be one of the rabbis of the Community Beth El, the house that Rabbi Marshall founded, where one can breathe in an atmosphere of dialogue with many fellow men and women and with a firm commitment to a more just and loving humanity.

I always say that interreligious dialogue is the voluntary endeavor that I chose for the rest of my life. Nobody compels me to do it. I don't carry it out on behalf of any institution. I, Silvina, look, "dive," study, get involved in interfaith dialogue, primarily to give greater meaning to who I am; and to bestow a purposeful characteristic to the function which, as a religious point of reference, I want to leave behind during my passage through the history of this country; but mainly for my children, Ariel and Ilán, so that they may savor and live with me the alternative of a better world, a united world, a world of possibilities and horizons.

In two separate voices: Francisco

Who am I?

I am Francisco Canzani and I was born in Uruguay. My mother is a practicing and committed Catholic. From my father, son of immigrants from Northern Italy, I received that "secular" accent that characterizes Uruguayans and that is part of their idiosyncrasy. I have a Doctorate in Law and Social Sciences, with a Civil Law specialty. For many years, while still living in my country, I juggled the practice of law with journalism and teaching. For nearly a decade, I have been teaching a course on Introduction to Ecumenical Theology at the University of Theology of Montevideo, my home town.

I am a layman in the sense that Christians give to the term, that is, I'm not a priest, but I am a committed Christian who lives his faith day after day in his surroundings, and who falls and rises as any other human being travelling in this world. Also I'm a consecrated layman. I felt the call of God to consecrate my life in order to make his Word a reality.

As a child I received a Catholic education at school and in my parish and later on, when I was a teenager, I became a member of the Focolare. The Focolare Movement (also known as the Work of Mary), one of the movements born in the twentieth century within the Catholic Church, has the countenance of the post-Vatican II church:[2] a leading role for the laity, a commitment to building a better world, the experience of brotherhood with all human beings and therefore the idea of dialoguing "to the nth degree."

It is from the spirituality and the experience of Focolare, from the charism of Chiara Lubich, its founder, that I explain my personal commitment to interreligious dialogue and, more specifically, to Jewish-Christian understanding. More generally, I am committed to the daily effort of building bridges with people of diverse religious confessions and convictions, hoping to give my contribution to the construction of a truly fraternal human family.

The experience of Chiara Lubich and the Focolare Movement has been decisive in my life. The call of Jesus to unity, "Father, may they all be one" (John 17:21) is my calling. In fact, it's not just my call, it is the call of all Christians. The search for the unity of the Church—the path of ecumenism—cuts across our life and our action. According to Chiara Lubich, interreligious dialogue is also part of the road to a united world in which we are all brothers and sisters. This phrase, "That all may be one," Chiara said, entails "all," really "all." Being children of one Father embraces Christians, and includes, perhaps mysteriously, all believers, as well as people of

---

2. Cf. Address of John Paul II at the Focolare Movement headquarters in Rocca di Papa, Italy, on August 19, 1984 . The pope acknowledged in the Movement the features of the Church as they were articulated at the Second Vatican Council.

no religious affiliation seeking the good of each person and of society.

When I was very young I joined the Judeo-Christian Fellowship of Uruguay. There I had many Jewish friends: Rabbi Daniel Kripper, Raquel Satkin, Sonia Kirchheimer, and many more. I remember with great affection an elderly Jewish man, James Hazán, who taught me a great deal about the path of dialogue. He was about eighty years old when we met. We had to work together in various activities of the Fellowship. We even had to jointly represent it later on in an international event. The intensity with which James listened to me, the respect he had for my Christian identity, the esteem he showed for what I said, and his search to penetrate and understand our experience as Christians and Catholics showed me a very concrete dimension of what dialogue ultimately means.

I must also say that there were many Christians who taught me to love Judaism, the "homeland" of Jesus: from my Uruguayan Hebrew teacher, Teresa D'Auria, an extraordinary person, to Teresa Porcile, a great theologian and a colleague at one point in my life. If it is true that God calls us to life and to follow a path to fulfill it, it is also true that he gives us the proper companions and invites us to choose the places where our vocation can become dialogue with him and with others. This has been and, still is, my experience.

Today, I live in the capital of Argentina and I coordinate the work of the Focolare Movement in the province of Buenos Aires and in the Patagonia.

In two separate voices: Francisco

Why dialogue?

We have only had fifty years of Jewish-Catholic dialogue after centuries of misunderstandings, hostility, persecution.

I wondered—logically—if these 50 years of a tradition of dialogue would be sufficient to start writing something valuable about the journey that the Second Vatican Council in the declaration *Nostra Aetate*[3] made us undertake. And I reached my first conclusion: not only are we still babbling like infants attempting their first syllables, but a full understanding between our religious traditions seems very far off. However, this "babbling" contains the seeds of words, sentences, paragraphs, pages, and books. We have to start somewhere and I must say that, from the experience of Christians and Catholics, these 50 years have revolutionized our way of thinking and acting in relation to the Jews.

I say "in relation to the Jews" on purpose—although the phrase may sound a bit unfriendly, since I reject the language which uses, in a confrontational way, "you" versus "us," and implies people who barely tolerate each other. I do not say "the Jews" to leave them out of my life and the life of "us" Christians. I say "you" because I want to recognize you as persons: a people, a religious tradition, a family, with its own identity—strong, valid, different from mine. The lack of recognition of the otherness and the uniqueness of the other, of his or her identity, never works well with the idea of dialogue. Quite the contrary.

The two loyalties

Thus, to enter into dialogue we need to have this dual allegiance. The first is the loyalty we owe to the gifts that God gave us in our respective traditions, which for us Christians, became "letters and words" in a common, to a certain degree, heritage (the Hebrew Bible, the

---

3. The declaration *Nostra Aetate* (*Our Time*) was promulgated by Paul VI on October 28, 1965, during the Second Vatican Council. It is the Council's document that addresses the issue of relations of the Catholic Church to non-Christian religions. Number 4 of the declaration is devoted to the relations between the Church and Judaism. It will be cited hereafter as *Nostra Aetate*, or simply as "NA."

First or Old Testament), and also in the Gospels and in the Second or New Testament.[4]

Loyalty to what our history showed us, taught us and which was reflected in thousands of facts and memorable pages that make up the coherent whole that constitutes our tradition. "Without tradition there is no faith," says Tillard,[5] and I'm sure it is true.

Fidelity to our tradition involves more, something very difficult to understand from "outside" the borders of the Catholic Church, but that for us is a fundamental part of our identity. It is the body of the teaching that the Church has taught over the centuries about herself, about her relationship with humanity and the world. The Church calls it "Magisterium,"[6] because the Church — the assembly, the people that God formed — is

---

4. The Second Testament, which Christians commonly called the New Testament, is a collection of writings of the apostolic age (the first century of the Christian era, the period of life of the first 12 companions of Jesus). They are considered by Christians God's Word revealed. They are the Gospels (from the Greek word meaning "good news") of Matthew, Mark, Luke and John. They relate the sayings and deeds of Jesus, and his human journey from his birth to his death and resurrection. The Second Testament also includes the book of the Acts of the Apostles, which speaks of the life of the first communities of the followers of Jesus of Nazareth and the travels and work of Paul of Tarsus, a Jew who persecuted Christians and who became an "apostle of Jesus to the Gentiles." It also includes letters of the apostle Paul to different church communities (the first "assemblies" of the followers of Christ) in the Mediterranean area, other letters of the apostolic period attributed to the apostles Peter, John, James and Jude; and the letter to the Hebrews, by an unknown author. The last Book of the Second or New Testament is the Book of Revelation, attributed to the apostle John, which describes symbolically the vicissitudes of several early Christian communities in the Greco-Roman world and refers to the final events of history, the "end of time," the so-called "Eschatology." We will refer to the New Testament as the Second Testament ("ST").

5. J. M. R. Tillard, *Iglesia de iglesias, eclesiología de comunión*, Salamanca, Ed. Sígueme, 1991, p. 195.

6. The Church's Magisterium consists of all the documents that the Church's hierarchy (popes and bishops) and assemblies (councils, synods) have developed and promulgated throughout the centuries. It is a true teaching that guides Catholics when approaching the Sacred Scriptures and Tradition (cf. a Vatican II document, the dogmatic constitution *Dei Verbum* on Divine Revelation, numbers 7 to 10). For example, Vatican II documents are part of the Magisterium of the Church as well as the encyclical letters or the pastoral letters of the bishop of a diocese.

for its baptized members their *"magister"* meaning *teacher.* It is the faithfulness to our deep identity, built by God and our people during centuries of a loving relationship, that makes us who we are today. When Jews enter into dialogue with Catholic Christians, they know who they are talking to and what are the beliefs of those who are their "different" brothers.

The second loyalty is this: God made Christians live quite a peculiar experience. The circumstances of the followers of Jesus of Nazareth during their early years, decades and centuries, led them to incorporate an idea that was somewhat foreign to the culture to which they belonged. It is the idea of "universality." It is a controversial term. We could argue about its meaning, and whether this concept unites us or divide us. But now I would like to look at this concept—which, again, stemmed from experience rather than ideas—, that enlightened the life of the early Christians. Their openness to the world of paganism of their time offered them a dimension that we can now recognize as positive.

One could easily object that, by virtue of this concept, Christianity tried to impose itself universally by using the power of the sword and of blood, subjugating peoples, enforcing religious practices, starting crusades, etc. It is true.

But, at the same time, thanks to the maturity acquired over the centuries, the idea of universality has proved to be a good idea. It expresses fundamentally that we are all called to form a single human family,[7] to be "blood" brothers by virtue of being children of the same Father. The faithfulness to the project of universal brotherhood that God harbors for humanity—in Christian theology—encourages us to encounter the "other," with

---

7. Cf. *Lumen Gentium* 1. *Lumen Gentium* (Light of the nations) is one of the Second Vatican Council's four most important and authoritative documents (together with *Dei Verbum,* cited above). It is a dogmatic constitution on the Church: what the Church is, how it lives within herself and its relationship with the world. Its number 16 refers to the relations of the Church with non-Christian religions, first, with Judaism. It will be cited hereafter as "LG."

whom we must travel on a road that uses work and action ("dialogue") in order to understand and meet one another, and to build and strengthen affectionate and effective bonds.

Dialogue with anyone, from any belief or conviction, is cemented on these two loyalties, at least from our Christian perspective. John Paul II, in his encyclical letter *Redemptoris Missio*, always in reference to interreligious dialogue, said:

> Those engaged in this dialogue must be consistent with their own religious traditions and convictions, and be open to understanding those of the other party without pretense or close-mindedness, but with truth, humility and frankness, knowing that dialogue can enrich each side. There must be no abandonment of principles nor false irenicism, but instead a witness given and received for mutual advancement on the road of religious inquiry and experience, and at the same time for the elimination of prejudice, intolerance and misunderstandings.[8]

"A people beloved by God"

But why then is dialogue with the Jews so endearing for Christians? Just because Jesus was a Jew and his religious tradition and his praxis and liturgy was that of Israel? We know that the people of Israel "remains most dear to God, for God does not repent of the gifts He makes nor of the calls He issues,"[9] and the Gospel of John says unequivocally "for salvation comes from the Jews."[10]

Do Christians need dialogue with Judaism in order to be themselves? Why do they need the "well-cultivated olive tree" onto which the wild olive was grafted,"[11] in the popular image of Paul? The Church cannot forget

---

8. *Redemptoris Missio*, 56. Encyclical Letter of John Paul II of December 7, 1990. It will be cited hereafter as "RM."
9. LG 16.
10. Cf John 4:22.
11. See Romans 11:24.

that "she draws sustenance from the root of that well-cultivated olive tree onto which have been grafted the wild shoots, the Gentiles."[12]

Nostra Aetate reminds us that "since the spiritual patrimony common to Christians and Jews is thus so great, this sacred synod wants to foster and recommend that mutual understanding and respect which is the fruit, above all, of biblical and theological studies as well as of fraternal dialogues."[13] These are words that we can read with some lightness, but that marked a "before" and an "after" in the deep bond between Jews and Christians, at least from a Christian perspective. It is unacceptable for us Christians to not adequately value, or even worse, disparage this essential bond constitutive of our identity. Will more reasons be necessary to consider mutual understanding and dialogue with the Jews an essential part of our religious experience?

Undoing a way

Perhaps, yes. There is a reason, which in my personal opinion is not insignificant at all, albeit one of an historical, sociological and, eventually, junctural nature. Almost twenty centuries of contempt by the Christian world toward the Jews cannot be backtracked and undone from one day to the next. The seeds of anti-Semitism are still hidden in the depths of the hearts of many Christians and sometimes they seem to be getting ready to sprout. Can we afford to harbor those seeds in our hearts? The answer is clearly negative. It is essential to eradicate them, so that the contempt (and even hatred) of Jews that the Church documents deplore, condemn and consider sin, may not self-destruct us. "He's only harming himself who's bent upon harming another," says the old aphorism. This is a great truth, which we Christians must grasp.

---

12. See NA 4.
13. Ibid.

In two separate voices: Silvina

Why dialogue?

> Rabbi Hama son of Rabbi Hanina said: 'What is implied by the verse "Iron sharpens iron?" (Proverbs 27:17) It tells you that just as one piece of iron sharpens another, so two scholars sharpen each other's mind by discussion of the Law.' Rabbah bar Hana said: 'Why have the words of Torah been compared to fire, as it is said: "Is not my work like fire?" (Jeremiah 23:29) To tell you that just as fire does not burn alone, so the words of Torah will not last in an individual.'
>
> *Babylonian Talmud, Tractate Taanit, 7a*

I belong to a tradition that requires a minimum of ten people to recite the prayers that proclaim the sanctity of God; therefore, certain rituals and liturgical prayers can only be said by a congregation, a group of at least ten worshippers called a "minyan" in Hebrew.

I belong to a people that address God in the second person because prayer is a way of dialoguing: "Blessed are You, Lord, Sovereign of the Universe." I belong to a nation that survived exiles, expulsions and massacres because it was anchored in the concept of community: knowing that one can count on the other at all times and that, in turn, one is responsible for the other.

Study, rites of passage, prayers and important moments of the year are lived together with many others. There is no Judaism in solitude but in a "network of conversations," as Humberto Maturana said: some are loud, others ensue while sharing the same text and many result simply because of someone's presence.

The realm of words, of questions and their subsequent answers, are part of the historic-genetic memory of the Jewish people. Therefore, returning to the example of the Talmud previously quoted, in order to increasingly strengthen who I am, I need someone else to help me "sharpen," to "set me on fire," to sustain my being through his or her companionship and questioning. This is why when I was invited to write a book on the craft (pedagogy) of educating for dialogue, I asked the publisher immediately for an interlocutor, someone with whom to share ideas and passions as well as to rethink and question myself in the context of a world that sometimes appears too chaotic.

Dialogue, hope for healing

Today, dialogue is our hope for healing. Jews and Christians share territory in many countries of the world but the trauma of history and the gap spawned between us have not provided us so far with the serenity and the security to get closer to one another. Painful facts and persecution, which some Christian groups staged throughout history, supposedly in the name of God, reverberate in the collective memory of the Jewish people. Words and images hammer the soul, creating barriers that hinder a close relationship: deicide, usury, Marranos, inquisitions, expulsions, executions, crusades, desecrations and destruction of synagogues, isolation, edicts and decrees of confinement and confiscations, property seizure and land expropriations, mockery, stigmatization, mandatory exiles, derogatory distinctive garb, etc. How does one regain trust?

Several very important steps have been taken. It is fitting that my friend Francisco writes about Church documents, and I would like to mention a declaration contained in *Nostra Aetate*: "The Church decries hatred, persecutions, displays of anti-Semitism, directed against Jews at any time and by anyone."

That was a big step, a first open door to believe again in that "re-binding" that religion is essentially supposed to bring about. Afterward, Pope John Paul II presided over a Prayer of Forgiveness in the Jubilee Year of 2000, in which, referring to the people of Israel, he said: "We are deeply saddened by the behavior of those who in the

34

course of history have caused these children of yours to suffer, and asking your forgiveness we wish to commit ourselves to genuine brotherhood with the people of the Covenant."

This is another unique, historic and hopeful step. While the first text deplores the existing persecution, the second asks for forgiveness for past persecutions. This is a good start. However, dialogue grows not only because of documents and official statements by the highest authorities, although they are indispensable steps. Dialogue is not just proclaimed, much less imposed, but springs forth from the will of human beings, who, after having been separated, decide to try to build bridges between them. I believe in dialogue because as Anne Frank said in her later writings: I believe that people are really good at heart. I think that just as atrocities were committed throughout history, this new time gives humanity the opportunity to show that we can make our goodness prevail and experience a new era, where we do not have to triumph over the other to be whom we are.

Sharing the other's narrative

Dialogue, in my view, means not only shared spaces and encounters but the ability to speak *about* the other, *from* the perspective of the other. In our case, it would entail for Jewish educators to speak about Christianity from the Christian perspective and not from their own, and vice versa. When we will create more spaces to share "the other's narrative," when more Christians will know about Judaism and will spread it in their educational settings, and when more Jews will show what they know about Christianity by including it in their pedagogical conversation, then, I think, we will have accomplished our goal.

In this time of loneliness and selfishness, I dialogue to stop listening to my monologue, to receive the word of the others, and, as a result, to have the opportunity to be moved by them, to understand them, to criticize them, and to know them. Perhaps the day has come to reject the myth that a broken mirror brings bad luck and break the mirrors we have placed to look only at ourselves. There is something valuable to discover on the other side of the glass that, even today, is totally unknown to many.

Lessons along the way

This is the first stop along the way of our writing. We have just started and we need to share with our readers the decisions that we took while this book was taking shape. We first had the need to introduce and talk about ourselves as individuals. While we know that many readers will simply identify us by the Jewish or Christian positions we stand for, we are Silvina and Francisco, in the company of our attitudes, skills, thoughts and emotions. And it is very important to us that you know us.

So we wrote "in two voices" because each one, if you'll excuse the repetition, is one: with one's baggage and individuality. And this also makes clear that there will be sections of the book that we will write together, while other segments will be written separately in order to respect our perspectives and paradigms.

To speak about ourselves in the first person involves stepping out of ourselves, using words and content for what defines us, in order to return to our own being. When we become fully aware of who we are, we are then able to take responsibility for ourselves as well as for our acts and our words.

In fact, this book is also about ensuring our accountability, for ourselves and for our neighbors. For the sake of this, we need to begin "at home." No one can do this job for us. It belongs to each one of us, at every step of the way. That's why we write separately what dialogue means for each one, because we set out from different needs and we go to encounter the other from our own perspectives, dreams, fears and illusions. However, when reflecting upon a pedagogy, we will write together, because we both need it. In addition, in order to figure out ways of reaching out to the other, it will be vital to be together and experience it first in our own flesh. Here we go, then... enjoy it!

In unison: Silvina *and* Francisco

Why a pedagogy of dialogue ?

Human beings are the result of multiple interactions and factors. We are born neither good nor bad, neither petty nor generous, neither submissive nor combative. We come into the world to be etched by experiences, stories, footprints, myths, attitudes, perspectives, judgments and prejudices. The beliefs of our families, our social setting, such as our schools, the successful or futile interacting with people we value—all these gradually add up to whom we are.

We all know that it is impossible to be aware of all the elements that form our identity. But it is undeniable that we are the result of different building blocks that we have learned and assimilated. At times, we got accustomed to them; other times we were amazed. We accepted with resignation or we rebelled before certain positions. Life is a great learning opportunity. Everything is learned. Attitudes of dialogue and prejudices are learned, they do not happen naturally and spontaneously.

We therefore believe that we must step beyond the positions already reached in Jewish-Christian dialogue. Christians and Jews have gotten closer. After two thousand years we have been able to sit together at the table, to build trust, and to address each other as brothers and sisters.

But dialogue requires much more than just official documents that frame our actions; many people need to "unlearn" the road of stereotypes and fears in order to "re-learn" the possibilities that dialogue brings. It is a long path, perhaps, but indispensable. The "assurances" that the official documents convey, while supporting us and encouraging us, must be complemented with the concrete experience of the other.

Living side by side and listening to others in an unbiased way confers an ability to welcome them and to deepen our understanding of their reality and experience that no document can give us. From the moment children are in kindergarten, teachers insist upon the value of the word and of listening to the others. Thus we grow, learning that dialogue is a social, human value.

Today we need teachers and students of interreligious dialogue. We need methodologies and content. We need to conceptualize the experience already made, paving the way for many who are still afraid, suspicious, or who do not know where to begin.

We need to recover both the knowledge and the previous "ignorance," in order to place them in their proper perspective. We need to re-introduce the soul as part of the curriculum and consider hope as a human capacity. Interreligious dialogue is in many senses an unfinished business and as such, we have decided to address it to pass it on to future generations.

The word *dialogue*, in its popular sense, refers to a conversation between two people. But it actually means understanding "through" words. Our pedagogy begins thus before dialogue occurs. It originates inside each one, in the images prior to the encounter, in the exploration of doubts and threats, in the definition of certainties and questions.

We need to internalize the "words," which we will be expressing afterwards. We cannot go out with the intention of teaching anything, if we do not devote ourselves first to, reflexively, "learn ourselves." We must know who and what we are and how to be ready to reach out to the other. This is an essential premise in order to open up to and discover the other in his or her uniqueness.

Ironically, openness towards the other becomes vital in order to know ourselves deeply and to be anchored in our identity. Dialogue and identity are two concepts and two attitudes that fuel each other and make us grow personally and communally. We have a long way to go:

two thousand years of silence waiting to be repaired in minutes of truth and sincere fraternity. We are not as powerful as to believe that we can solve all the fractures and misunderstandings, but as people of faith, we will not stop trying. As the Talmud says, in tractate Avot 2:16, "It is not your responsibility to finish the work, but you are not free to desist from it either." Maybe we will not reach great goals, although it is difficult to define what a "great goal" may be. But Jesus himself reminds us that "Whoever can be trusted with very little can also be trusted with much" (cf. Luke 16:10, Matthew 25:23). The path of dialogue is itself already an achievement, both small and large, reached with much faith and hard work.

Many speak of interfaith dialogue in terms of "utopia," a word that does not describe the direction to follow. For us dialogue is definitely not a utopia. The etymology of the word, from the Greek ou (meaning "no") and topos (meaning "place") expresses a non-place, a space that does not exist. From our experience, we can say that that horizon of interfaith dialogue does exist, and it is possible and accessible. The only thing required is that we learn the ways to walk toward it and to integrate the ideas, which may be unrealistic for many, as our own goals and ideals.

Chapter 2

Reflections before Action

In unison: Francisco *and* Silvina

The role of educators in interreligious dialogue

A PEDAGOGY OF INTERRELIGIOUS DIALOGUE takes place when there are educators who believe in it. And we say "believe" because more than the development of teaching concepts and skills, the ability to transmit the universe that dialogue summons requires human beings who are challenged by emotions and convictions. People, who have responsible positions—religious representatives, leaders of youth groups, teachers, rabbis, priests, catechists, professors—should understand that the ability to dialogue is an attitude towards others when they represent what I am not, and yet, without them, "I would not be able to be."

We chose to cross the threshold of dialogue from the interfaith dimension, first, because it is the field to which we are dedicated as educators, and secondly, because religious communities in this time of globalization remain places of preservation of social and spiritual values. They are points of reference where an ethical worldview has not yet been compromised.

Religious traditions, each one in its own way, uphold the values of social justice, equality, love and holiness, which at times this world has decided to ignore. Reality often assaults us with grisly social images, which seem to leave no way out and, in the face of so much distress, faith communities continue to be a reliable stronghold, a

protected space where spirituality remains an unequivo-
cal value.

Every religious community, in one way or another,
lives the so-called *golden rule*: "Do not do unto others
what you do not want others to do unto you. Do unto
others as you would have them do unto you." It is within
this context that we can then teach commitment to the
others, mutual love, empathy and social responsibility.
That's why we say that it is from the religious field that
we want to radiate out to other human life structures
where people develop. A strong formation in the ability
to dialogue and to respect the other will improve our
family and work relationships and even our political positions.

This book has been written for all men and wom-
en who are involved in all areas of education, whether
formally or informally: in communities and parishes,
schools and youth groups, religious movements, recre-
ational and cultural associations, and universities. We
also hope that this text may reach not only those whom
society recognizes as educators, but everyone because
we can all have positive and formative influence in our
own environment: in our families, our jobs, our group
of friends.

Every moment in life is a suitable opportunity to sow
understanding and respect for others. We all bring positive values but also prejudices to our daily conversations.
We all, therefore, can be students and teachers in this
path of dialogue.

Characteristics of our societies

A paper on "Social transformation through inter-
culturalism: achievements and challenges," presented
by Cristina Calvo in May 2011 in New York, delineated
some categories connected to the economy that cause its
ethical emptying. These might well be applied to matters in which interreligious dialogue can give a major
contribution.

"Human relations have been reduced to a mere exchange of equivalents."

Strategic thinking, such as "if we are to take the time to give, we need to have our reward ensured," makes it difficult, at times, to place ourselves in a context of exchange and reciprocity, if our profit is not made explicit in advance. When we are prisoners of this kind of thinking we miss the opportunity to benefit from rewards, which are physically invisible but spiritually essential.

In the language of dialogue, reaching out to the others and the will to access their world may not have an equivalent, immediate or even measurable reaction. We enter into dialogue when we dare to break the logic of opportunism and the pathological need to feel always that we are winners. On the contrary, the less we aspire to "beat" the others, but to walk along with them, the more enriched and victorious we turn out to be. We don't "exchange," as if we were merchandise or property, but we share spaces of humanity that we need to decode in order to approach the others and ultimately to further recognize ourselves.

"The sphere of rationality has been reduced to that of calculability."

We would like to draw attention to two words of this proposition by Cristina Calvo:[1] rationality and calculability. The only thing that seems valid is what we can calculate, measure, predict, anticipate and thus control by virtue of the logic of reason. It is true that with calculations and reason we can reach verifiable results, but is it enough for a human to live in a "spreadsheet" format and miss the beauty of understanding a world in the company of quests and mysteries to solve through experiences and emotions? True, things are priced according to the rules of a certain market of supply and demand;

---

1. Delivered in a lecture given by Cristina Calvo in a conference entitled "Convivencia plural en la Argentina" on May 9, 2011 in New York, cosponsored by the Argentinean Ministry of Foreign Affairs and the New School of New York City.

but what discipline can measure the value of hope, belief, gratitude and awe?

We do not deny at all the value of the quantifiable, but boldly insist that there is another world, as rich and complex as consumption's, which deals with an inseparable aspect of the human being, which is constitutive of his more intimate humanity and is formed and educated by values, not by prices.

Dialogue does not require contracts that guarantee a proper functioning of the transaction, but rather requires people of good will who want to carry out actions to ensure the dignity of others, without tabulations or labels, but with the freedom to want to be and let oneself be in the other.

"Trust, a relationship, has been reduced to reputation."

"I go if it's good for my status." "I go if it's advantageous." "I go if the other is prestigious and therefore I will stand out." These types of phrases have left the value of trust without too many advocates. We propose here that dialogue requires, as a basic premise, even prior to the encounter, conditions of trust, faith in the other, with the other and in oneself, as well as not feeling made vulnerable by the presence of the other. It is an a priori condition that doesn't involve titles or credits, but the tranquility of knowing that we are respected, welcomed and well regarded by those who are before us. Dialogue does not confer a certain rank in a promotion ladder. It is certainly an adventure that makes us reach for the infinite and sense that we are building bridges that unite us with the others and bring us closer to heaven, to the same project that the Creator has for this world.

"Finally, happiness was reduced to utility."

Some people ask us: why do you dialogue, what's the point of it? Why waste time in something useless, if this world is beyond repair? Why dialogue, if I already have a defined identity? We attempt to give some answers based on our many shared moments.

We don't know whether dialogue is useful in the same terms that we might rate a computer or an appliance. What is nonnegotiable is that dialogue contributes to our happiness. Or put in another way, dialogue is for us absolutely useful because it strengthens us, it changes our view of ourselves, the others, society and even history. Dialogue improves the quality of our relationships, the contact with our children and students, because it shapes our hopes and makes us more careful and accountable for our words, because it refines our sensibilities and makes us feel worthy of the faith we profess. Could we call it happiness? Yes, we think so.

The art of inviting the other

Perhaps one of the most overlooked concepts of our time, which might contribute the most to the vision we seek to share with our readers, has to do with hospitality. The educator Giuseppe Milan explained the idea of hospitality as an art, the art of inviting the other, in a lecture given at the Fourth Symposium of Judeo-Christian Dialogue held at Mariapolis Lia, O'Higgins, Argentina, in 2011.

Inviting the others supposes first that we have something valuable and appealing to offer to them. At the same time, it involves the desire to make room for them in our own space and consider them as a legitimate Thou—in the categories of the philosopher Martin Buber—, a "thou" who can never be regarded as an object (an "it-ness"). When we show that there is room for this "You," the art of hospitality begins to unfold. Humility, a necessary condition for establishing a true encounter, means experiencing one's own emptiness and being aware that we alone are not complete. Being humble, writes Paulo Freire, simply means "to be able to feel and know oneself as a man like any other."

Giuseppe Milan suggested two metaphors: the humble is like a traveler, and the arrogant like a landowner sitting in his mansion. The hospitality of the humble is characteristic of people who search, who are dynamic in their search and thus trigger the encounter: they desire and are concerned with meeting the other, and as a result, the encounter takes place. They are different from those who, sitting in their mansions, open their coffers to give out part of their wealth. Hospitality has to do less with providing what we have in our households than with sharing our needs, making of this encounter our common roof.

To accept is to carry along, to contain, to embrace. The Latin root, *accipere* means "to conceive, to give life." When we are accepted and welcomed, we relive the experience of our birth and we return to be conceived in a world of fraternity and reciprocal love. It is hospitality without conditions, without stigma or any strategy to prevent, discriminate or isolate any distinctive feature of the other.

And how is this art taught? By putting it into practice and inviting others to be part of this journey, an adventurous journey in search of new realities and colors to complement ours, in order to paint our somber spaces and give rise to new shades, which we, alone, would have never discovered.

We will really be mentors of hospitality, embrace it, and welcome it if we treat others as worthy subjects, with their stories and beliefs, making room for them within ourselves; not to change ourselves but to accompany each other side by side, on this journey of our shared lives.

A toolbox

The mission is clear. The intention is defined. All who gather around this text agree: we want dialogue and we are committed to it. However, such a complex human process does not end with the mere definition of the goal. Naturally, we do not approach someone who represents the "other" without any preconceptions and without fear. Dialogue is built with concrete tools. And we speak of tools, not weapons, because in order to enter into dialogue we need to be "disarmed" and rid ourselves of anything that can harm the other—and ultimately ourselves—and surrender to the battle of edification.

Let us open our hands to receive these tools that will allow us, step by step, to venture into the encounter with each other. They are tools to ensure our integrity and our neighbor's. Each one of them is a phase that we have already walked through up until this present moment in which we are together writing a book on the pedagogy of dialogue.

It took us a long time, because dialogue requires perseverance, commitment and some risk. After having lived this process, we feel that we should tell others what we have learned, especially those others who are searching for a more united world.

Chapter 3

Reflections on Trust

Two separate voices: Silvina

Trust: a necessary condition to start

EVERYONE KNOWS THAT TRUST must exist between people in order for them to have meaningful relationships. What do we mean by trust? How is it generated? How do we know we are not confused or seeing a mirage instead of reality? Who has not been disappointed with relationships that left us exposed, where we opened our heart and the other betrayed us? How can we leave that safe nest made out of those who know me and protect me?

These thoughts may explain the fear we have of responding to something as sensitive, as human and inexplicable as trust—faith in the other. How much we wished we were able to define exactly what faith is so as to walk on solid ground! Even so, I must go beyond the difficulties and rely on my own experiences of dialogue, those that worked and still do, and those that failed. I learned something from all of them about this first tool we call "trust."

At least for me, it is impossible to get close to another if the feeling that I have is that I will fall into the abyss or that I am putting myself at risk. Trust or lack of trust are indicators of the degree of emotional fragility with which we perceive ourselves.

Trust is knowing that one's integrity will not be violated, that one's own being will not be insulted, that beyond the differences, there is a sacred space that cannot be infringed upon. That confidence allows me to know that I don't have to stop being myself in order to be listened to or accepted, that I need not hide in front of the person that is next to me, because the depth of my being is not being questioned. Human relationships depend on trust. And I insist, trust is not something that comes with our human nature; it is something that must be built by each one of us.

The initial contact

Trust is connected to respect. If I approach the others with whom, knowing and accepting their differences, then it is likely that the others will not feel threatened. Language (verbal communication) builds trust. So does body language: the way we greet one another and look at each other, our facial expression, are as important as the words that we speak. There is an initial contact in dialogue, which is not specified or defined: one either feels secure or insecure. Knowing that we are respected paves the way with confidence for the encounter with the other.

Although the external format of the encounter may be guaranteed in an institutional framework for dialogue or in the context of a day of peace or an international seminar, the first meeting is crucial. When we approach the others, we should ask ourselves: Do they engender trust? Do I feel comfortable? Is the ground firm? I am speaking about that first moment, which is more intuitive, more primitive, if I may say. It is sensed through a "scent" that human nature gives us to save us from an attack.

Trust as a process

Next, there is a deeper dimension of trust that ought to be nourished and cared for. Once we establish a relationship, we must be thoughtful not only of the content of our exchanges but also of the gestures that reinforce our trust in others and our desire to be trustworthy.

We need to clarify something: from the outset, when we speak of trust we are not referring to a strategy. We cannot disguise ourselves as confident or reliable people in order to conclude an assignment or to appear inclusive before the public. Trust is a process of human interconnection which unfolds with experience. Therefore, sporadic encounters of dialogue among people who do not know each other can certainly contribute interesting theoretical ideas and good speeches, but they do not build dialogue, at least not the concept of dialogue that we consider here.

Trust is thus generated by a thorough effort of opening spaces of mutual understanding. Behind the position that each one represents — in our case, a religious one, but it may be of any kind — there is a person, a story, a home, dreams, family, etc.

I remember that my first encounter with the Focolare Movement, at an institutional level, was when my son Ariel, his friend Natasha and I were privileged to be invited as Jews to participate in a youth event, the Supercongress for Unity in Rome in 2002.

The Argentine group was very large, about 120 young people and 4 coordinators, all of them Christians, who would travel with us. The first thing I felt was the need to look at them face to face, greet them and chat before we got on the plane. I needed to discover the persons with whom I was to share an experience, in order to then enter into dialogue with them, who were different and Christians. And so it happened. One afternoon, during an improvised snack, without too many chairs to sit on, three Jews got together with about 20 Catholics in order "to sow trust." We greeted each other warmly; we sat on armchairs, on the floor, anywhere we found a place, in order to chat; we shared about who we were, what school we attended; we joked and shared soft drinks. All of this may seem trivial, but it is not. It was important and necessary. We were equal and different. We spoke the same language and everyone his or her own.

Afterwards, we wanted to get to know each other better. So, we went together to the event, in the midst of many cultures, religions, colors and odors. We learned to take care of and listen to each other, to have fun together without holding back our opinions and ideas. But this happened because we took some time first, which guaranteed that no one would be in danger, that together we were safe.

And so I could tell you about every experience of sincere dialogue. Dialogue does not begin at a conference table but when we open our home, the sanctuary, the family, the stories, the humanity of each one, in order to later on enter into the challenging field of religion.

From here on, I venture to say that trust generates a current of affection. And assuming that we cannot love what we do not know, we could say that trust begins with mutual knowledge, that is, to want to know the other and to let the other get to know us, with sincerity of heart.

Finally, I would like to say that these are processes that take time. After walking the first step, in general we test trust and check whether it holds. There will be no progress in dialogue unless mutual trust gets stronger. And the closer we are, the more fragile is the terrain of the encounter with the other. It is not conquered ground, it is a dimension that depends all the time on our actions, our interventions and words. The deeper the dialogue, the subtler the need for trust.

When will we know that we have achieved trust? I'm sorry to say that it cannot be reached completely, but it is strengthened or weakened according to what each one contributes. It is not a good that is acquired but a capacity that must be cultivated continuously.

A look at the sacred text

My dear friend, the priest Francesco Ballarini once wrote me this beautiful sentence: "Each person is a mystery whom I have to come close to, as Moses did when he started to approach the burning bush and God asked him to take off his sandals first." In order to answer him, I returned to the text of Exodus:

> There the angel of the LORD appeared to him as fire flaming out of a bush. When he looked, although the bush was on fire, it was not being consumed. So Moses decided, "I must turn aside to look at this remarkable sight. Why does the bush not burn up?" When the LORD saw that he had turned aside to look, God called out to him from the bush: Moses! Moses! He answered, "Here I am."
>
> *(Exodus 3:2–4)*

There are many lessons here for those who want to practice dialogue:

At first, what happens to Moses happens to most of us. We walk in our realities, lost in our own selves, often ignoring the wonders that surround us, to the point of becoming blind to the presence of others and other things.

Moses, like many others in his time, was walking around the desert and he stopped. He did not take for granted the presence of a bush, a small shrub, quite insignificant in a desert. Nor did he take as natural the fact that it was on fire but did not burn up. ??? He stopped. He took his time in front of a reality that was outside of him. He dedicated time and space in his routine in order to understand what he had in front of him.

Then comes the call: "Moses, Moses." God calls to the man bearing a name, because encounters occur in this way, with the intention of addressing and questioning the other. And we must know the name in order to do that. And not just once but twice, "Moses, Moses" as if to say: "I confirm my eagerness to call you, because you're the one that interests me." Lastly, once this first scene, which guarantees the possibility of a dialogue, takes place, Moses replies: "Here I am." "Here I am," ready with all my being for this encounter to happen. I proved it when I stopped to observe what was around me. There, I felt that there was also the desire of the other side to get closer, because I was called twice by my own name. And then, of course, I'm here!

Who could resist such an invitation, such a challenge? The other, whoever turns up on our way — or our desert — is like the burning bush, is part of a daily reality toward which we sometimes are indifferent, perhaps to shield ourselves from pain, perhaps not to venture in ways we cannot fully control. Instead, when we stop, we slow down the march and we modify our safe routines.

As a result, realities appear before our eyes never before seen or registered: they are the others, with their wealth of fire that does not burn, but that illuminates and gives heat without destroying. The others, then, are like those small shrubs, common people, without prestigious positions, just like you and me, like many other people of good will who are by the roadside waiting to be found, looked at, and recognized, in order to give of themselves.

But the bush also took a transcendent step: it called. It took the time to name us, and in that name, it bestowed our identity and our rights. This book is like those stops that Moses made on his journey, to move toward the wonder and the awareness of being both found and finder at the same time.

We know that if we get close we will not burn because the fire that we have is the fire of the soul searching for nourishment in the souls of the others, who are nothing more than portions of God in each human being.

This beautiful passage from Exodus continues: "Do not come any closer," God said. "Take off your sandals, for the place where you are standing is holy ground." (Exodus 3:5)

I would recommend some reflections on this verse. The first involves removing the shoes. In this action, concrete for Moses and symbolic for us, I find infinite wisdom. In order to get close to your neighbor, you must shed your security systems and what connects you to the profound sensations of having the ground beneath your feet. Even more, you must get rid of any element that facilitates your escape, because to go near the other you must accept your "nakedness," staying clear of your preconceptions and strategies, developing the capacity to get in touch with the most elementary sensations; you must lose your balance in order to step toward the other.

And why? Because the ground on which you stand is holy. And it has nothing to do with the built sanctuaries. It means that any surface can be sacred when we consecrate it to the encounter with the other in any moment of life.

The teacher Rabbi Marshall Meyer taught: "I think that every person in the world, at one time or another, puts his or her faith and trust in another individual, and that only a select few are able to accept the consequences of such a commitment." Accepting the commitment means to make a pledge with our neighbors to walk our separate ways while sharing always the same horizon. Accepting the commitment means to compromise the course by accepting the other, which is ultimately accepting oneself and the best way to make room for God's blessing.

In two separate voices: Francisco

Trust: gratuitousness and responsibility

It is difficult to speak of trust, the tool for dialogue now at hand, without drawing upon personal experience. We have all experienced what it means to give and to receive trust. It is a strong, true experience that can be lived in any human relationship and that is necessary for the relation to be such. Without trust, we never go beyond the mere façade of a relationship and this does not amount to much. Trust makes us grow, allows us to express ourselves fully, and compels us to look for the most authentic within us in order to give it to the one who trusts us.

It's this perspective that allows the path of dialogue to develop. Without it, we walk and grope around aimlessly because the interlocutor, the other, will always be a stranger for us, someone to be wary of and to keep an eye on. The same will befall the other who is in front of us.

For instance, I was organizing a Judeo-Christian event together with a group of Jewish friends. It involved detailed work that demanded great concentration and precision. I was at that time very young, and those who worked with me were older and very competent in their field. I remember how sincerely they listened to me. I felt clearly that they trusted me with the task at hand and this made me want to rise to the occasion in order to refine my contribution. In particular, I remember an elderly Jewish gentleman who listened to each of my interventions with great interest. I felt his trust toward me and this encouraged me to make sure that every word I said was adequate. This person brought the best out of me; his gaze made me want to be better, prevented me from being too quick to judge, and opened up a space of freedom and responsibility where I could express myself.

Trust is the big space where everyone offers who they are, expressing it without hesitation, knowing that it will be respected and appreciated, and that appreciation and respect will generate more appreciation and respect, causing the relationship to reach new heights. Trust allows us to reveal ourselves as we are, with our personal and religious values, without fear of being misunderstood.

Wherever trust reigns, every word and gesture achieve meaning beyond their purpose because the giver and the receiver of trust spontaneously and gradually respond better to the other's requests and needs.

The positive outlook

Trust entails an act of faith in the possibilities of the others, beyond their appearances. It is sort of a positive "outlook" that helps us and the other to be open. It is a perspective "with faith" that points out the interior of the others and knows how to find valuable things in them in order to highlight them. It is an attitude that encourages the others, inspires them to aim always higher, and allows them to broaden their views and their ability for understanding and for altruism. Trust can bring about a fraternal human bond and a space for dialogue.

For instance, a Jewish friend that I went to Biblical Hebrew classes with invited the whole group to her house. She introduced her family to us. I remember very well her mother-in-law: she was a survivor of the Holocaust who shared with us episodes of her long and painful life. In the simple and confident words of this elderly woman, I understood as never before the horrors of the Nazi extermination camps. A bond of trust was created that allowed her to unlock the depth of her story and allowed us to participate existentially in one of the strongest moments of her life, making it, somehow, our own.

Trust is deserved and is given

It is true that one must be worthy of trust, and it is also true that it can be freely given. Trust allows us to accept the others without the need to fully understand them or even know everything about them. As the example of the elderly lady shows, she did not know us well, but she still trusted us. Her trust made it an unforgettable moment.

Therefore, the free gesture of giving trust and the effort we make in order to deserve it are like the two sides of the same coin. They create the stage for the actors of dialogue to express themselves honestly, aware of their reality and the other's. Trust makes dialogue take place, because it opens one to express what one thinks and feels, and to receive what the other thinks and feels, without fear of being despised.

Authentic dialogue thrives on trust and to the extent that it grows and deepens, it engenders more trust. In some measure, trust precedes true dialogue, but is also the result of true dialogue. When trust is freely granted and received responsibly, it spawns more dialogue and dialogue builds more trust. It is a virtuous circle that we must always be vigilant not to break. It is subtle and delicate, but when fully consolidated, it is a guarantee of growth and of stable and productive encounters.

Lessons along the way

While writing our concrete recommendations for bringing about trust, we decided to include a reflection that had come up when we tried to answer the question: Why is it so hard to trust one another? And we reached the following hypothesis: Jews and Christians are asymmetric in history and theology. They possess their own narrative of events according to their own perspective and learned tradition. The fact that Jesus was Jewish and that Christian liturgy includes fixed First Testament readings, makes the bond of Christians with Jews depart from a different point than that of the Jews towards Christians. There is a connection with and a mention of Jewishness in Christian life which does not exist in Jewish history and liturgy, because thus were the facts of history. In the collective imagination, the Judaism of Jesus is in the "daily agenda" of the Christian.

On the other hand, a large percentage of the Jewish population of the world lives in countries with Christian majorities, where the liturgical calendar, the symbology, the gastronomy, and the messages of the media about Christianity are dominant. In other words, Jews and Christians, when dialoguing, are connected by different factors that put them at different starting points.

We consider now another type of asymmetry. Sometimes you hear Christian people say that they are tired of being pointed at by Jews as the perpetrators of the Inquisition or the Crusades. This keeps them away from any closeness, because they do not feel they should be the ones to apologize for those periods of history. Similarly, some Jews believe that dialogue with Christians is fruitless because, despite all official documents to the contrary, Christians still accuse them of being responsible for "deicide" and this is an unbridgeable gap when sitting at the table.

All of this is true. Indeed, we have historical asymmetrical power relations, of winners and losers throughout history. And we can't turn a blind eye to this reality. While the world moves ahead at steps once thought to be inconceivable to the human mind, on faith-related topics, our steps are slower and, in all honesty, why not say it, more suspicious; because many in the name of faith have tainted their holiness by manipulating the faithful and that has left a mark difficult to erase today. This historical and theological asymmetry is a fact that we need to deal with, since it is unchangeable. But perhaps today we find other historical possibilities. For a long time, the triumphalism of one religion over the others marked the spheres of power and domination. Reverend Bruce Feiler[1] quotes Dr. Richard Wood when he said: "What's happened, at least in theological circles, is that triumphalism is dead. People aren't even asking the question. Of course there are a bunch of people who haven't figured this out yet. But they will."

It is true, the time has passed when the survival of the Jews depended on the failure of Christians to dominate them and the power of Christians to control their land. This long era called "triumphant" has ceased to be the code on which Christians and Jews base their existence. And when we will be able to recognize this, we will understand that we can respond with a position of

1. Abraham, *A journey to the Heart of the Three Faiths*, New York, USA, Harper Collins Publishers Inc., 2002

existential symmetry to this theological and historical asymmetry.

Today we recognize that we are equal, that we can live out our choices freely and the presence of the other does not threaten our integrity. And we are symmetric because history made us understand that the hierarchies and the "less than holy" battles, in our opinion, weakened and impoverished us. Today, people of faith, Jewish and Christian, are able to sit at the same table and we believe that many, in the bottom of their hearts, are longing to do the same.

In unison: Francisco *and* Silvina

Specific attitudes that build trust

The recommendations that follow are the result of our personal experience. They are attitudes or gestures that brought about trust in the other and that proved to be applicable to other encounters. The first moment is crucial. Two strangers, who come from different fields to an encounter "between different people," begin to know one another. There, body language plays an important role. How do we greet the person? Do we start the greeting or wait for the other to come to us? To do this we must find out whether the person we'll meet can shake hands—whether male or female—whether his or her culture or level of religiosity allows for a kiss or a hand shake. To start the dialogue, as we said in previous chapters, we must first prepare ourselves beforehand by getting to know the religious tradition and the customs of those whom we will meet.

We will say our names, we will introduce ourselves: How? Which words will be safe? How are we going to appear in front of the others? How much space do we leave them to make themselves known?

Small and simple gestures such as eye contact, nodding or returning a smile can put aside fears and suspicions. There are formal presentations and others that are more casual. We'll have to decide the best way to start a connection. Attitudes, even if minimal, can open or close doors. We should pay attention to the level of friendliness and kindness that we have when relating to others; the consistency between what we say or do in public and what we do and say in private, and between our words and what our voice, face and body communicate; the way we show our interest in the other; the attitude we have when listening as opposed to intending only to be listened to.

How often do we use "I" and how often "we"? How do we react to a disagreement? Do we get confused? Do we seek ways of negotiation? Do we shut down? What will be the focus of our dialogue: ourselves and our suggestions, or do we want to focus on getting to know the life and the opinions of the other? How do we manifest our doubts about the other? How do we make explicit the desire to maintain this relationship?

Let's not forget: we are much more than our particular position or role; we are much more than representatives of a movement or a religion, more than a religious or theological authority. We are human beings full of nuances and our relationships become tender when one abandons protocol to enter the realm of the interpersonal, that sensitive space that tells us without words whether the one across the table trusts us or not.

Interfaith dialogue, as we have said, takes place among people. Two people who start dialoguing don't always feel empathy for one another. Dialogue thus cannot be forced. We insist, the personal characteristics of each one either will facilitate or make dialogue more difficult. We must find the trust in each other to keep going forward.

Lessons along the way

When we defined the first topic that we were going to develop, we realized that the word trust had different connotations for each one of us. The reason is simple: we all bring to the table different experiences that drew us near or estranged us from others. We could not write a text in "unison " because each one had to be able to find the necessary conditions to enter into dialogue. That's why the beginning of this chapter is "in two separate voices," with the hope that each reader will add to this thread one's own voice and experience.

We cannot define trust universally, because it depends on multiple factors. When we made the decision to start writing separately, we learned a great lesson: we must recognize our own parameters, those that give us security to meet the other, but we must also know that maybe the other does not have the same ones. This requires humility and patience: when one is ready, is the other ready in the same way? We are not always credible before the other, our timing is not always the same as the other's. We should never despair but know how to keep going.

Sometimes you invite home someone with a friendly intention and that invitation may not be acknowledged in the time and manner we would consider adequate. What do we do? Do we close the door? Do we get angry? Do we judge the other negatively? Perhaps these would be the quickest and least thoughtful attitudes. But interfaith dialogue has other rhythms and sometimes silence or ostracism denote less ill will than difficulty, fear, and insecurity. What can we do in this situation? We can keep on inviting them home and opening doors without preconceived notions, trying to understand that each one has a different way of elaborating these processes.

Returning to our method, once we wrote our own views on the subject, we understood that the tools and resources that each one of us had available to build trust were enriching to both. That's why we wrote the last part of the chapter "in unison," together, because company is always good when learning and because when you share what you learn, everything takes another dimension. When our understanding and our objective focus on discovering ourselves and the other in order to engender dialogue, then every step we take is a new lesson to be learned, each person we meet becomes a teacher. Silences also teach, as well as successes, frustrated situations, anxieties and objectives achieved. Everything is educational material to put on the working table.

Chapter 4

Reflections on Sensible, Mature, and Committed Listening

In two voices and in unison

Because nobody listens when alone...

W E ARE ENTERING STEP by step into this endless forest of dialogue. In this chapter, we intend to focus on the skills and tools that must be developed in order to learn how to listen. Perhaps since hearing is a sense that most have from birth, sometimes it may seem inconsequential to think of something that we do "automatically." We all know that listening goes beyond simply capturing sound waves; it sets off the possibility to pay attention and to notice that someone is talking to us. Still, these approaches are insufficient because if it were that simple, we would not constantly reflect upon how to be aware of the value of listening and the tools for teaching and learning about it.

As we were writing this book, we set two challenges for ourselves. The first was to write together most of this chapter. That is, to experience ourselves firsthand what we will explain throughout this text: knowing what to say, when to be quiet, how to give space to the other, how to accept differences and how to incorporate them into the text, while still expressing our opinions freely. Our second goal in this part of the book is to analyze different sacred texts in Judaism and Christianity that serve as examples, as the foundational anchors for what we want to share.

In unison: Francisco *and* Silvina
"Listening" in our sacred texts

The question we had when we started to undertake this chapter was: where do we start developing this topic? The decision we made was this: we would put ourselves to the test by studying together passages from the Hebrew Bible and the Gospel to see whether we found in them a message about the ability to listen. The challenge was encouraging; for the first time each one was going to teach the other and we had to open our minds and our hearts to those teachings. So, this chapter was born through an exchange of words and listening.

Stories of the Origins - Genesis

Our conversation about listening went back to its origins and its obstacles. Consider this argument: sometimes we don't listen because we don't want to or we don't know how to, and other times because nobody is speaking.

These thoughts led us to the text in Genesis about the beginning of humanity:[1]

> Cain spoke to Abel his brother. And when they were in the field, Cain rose up against his brother Abel and killed him. (Genesis 4:8)

Thus the first brothers begin a story that, with different nuances and settings, will be repeated up until our times.

Cain and Abel are the first pair of brothers. If we read closely, we see that in the cited verse, a very important detail is missing: "Cain spoke to Abel his brother." It is not reported what he told him. There was no word

1. It is notable that in Christian Bibles, this verse says, "Cain told his brother Abel: *'let's go outside'* and when they were in the field, Cain rose up against him and killed him." (*Biblia de Jerusalén*, Bilbao, Ed. Desclée de Brouwer, 1975. There is a note in this text regarding this verse which clarifies that the words "let's go outside" are omitted in Hebrew). In the edition *Biblia del Peregrino* (Bilbao, EGA—Mensajero, 1993) the translation of the omitted text in Hebrew is *"let's go to the field."* We are using here the original Hebrew text.

or reflection, not even a discussion, but silence. And it was then that Cain rose up against his brother and killed him.

Because when there is no space for communication between two people, the other becomes a danger that threatens our very existence. When there is no text, there is no way to know about the other in order to get acquainted with him. The silence between the two brothers in Genesis challenges us not to repeat history.

An action alone unfolded because there were no meaningful words: the devastating violence to annihilate Abel. Cain might have thought that there was no room for two different people. The story between these brothers was born with a discrepancy, a difference that needed to be discussed or explained. Did Cain try to say something meaningful to his brother?

If we go back to the story, God regards Abel's offering but not Cain's. Was this the situation that caused the silence between the brothers? Would humanity have been changed, had they been encouraged to take the time to speak, tell, question, anything other than remaining silent? Was there silence or was there a word not received by the other?

The other exists, "happens," when there is a mediation through words and the act of listening is created between one and the other, linked by the speech. One speaks, the other listens; one shows that he or she exists and the other shows, by listening, that the one who speaks is someone that matters, worthy of listening to.

Pierre Legendre,[2] in his book *The Fashioning of Western Man*, referring to man's search for a reason to live, emphasizes the value of the word as constitutive of that reason: "In the course of our bloody history, the following recurs everywhere: when humans no longer put up with the word, the slaughter reappears." It is therefore important to use words, words of question, of consensus, of dissent, of research, of curiosity, words that will abide

2.   Buenos Aires-Madrid, Amorrortu Editores, 2008, p. 17.

in the other who listens to them and receives them. That is why Genesis desperately cries out that the first death (between brothers no less), was preceded by the lack of words and the lack of listening.

Martha and Mary, two paradigms of the Gospel

> Now as they went on their way, he entered a certain village, where a woman named Martha welcomed him into her home. She had a sister named Mary, who sat at the Lord's feet and listened to what he was saying. But Martha was distracted by her many tasks; so she came to him and asked, "Lord, do you not care that my sister has left me to do all the work by myself? Tell her then to help me." But the Lord answered her, "Martha, Martha, you are worried and distracted by many things; there is need of only one thing. Mary has chosen the better part, which will not be taken away from her." (Luke 10:38–42)

In this episode, Martha and Mary symbolize, in the tradition of the Church, two aspects of existence: acting and listening, both valid and necessary. Jesus comes to the house of the sisters and each of them adopts a very different, but equally active and positive attitude. Martha works to serve Jesus, Mary is apparently doing nothing, just listening to him as he speaks.

Martha confronts Jesus and asks him to correct Mary. For Martha, the most important thing is to take action immediately and she expects Mary to help with the housework. Martha works hard in order to welcome Jesus, to make him feel comfortable, but she doesn't realize that her activism is depriving her of the only thing that is "needed." Jesus praises Mary's attitude above Martha's. "Mary has chosen the better part, which will not to be taken away from her." What does Mary do? She listens, she just listens to Jesus. The rabbi of Nazareth, as many called him, qualifies "listening" as the only thing that is needed. Listening to the word. Jesus praises the ability to "listen" as the attitude required for any action.

This Gospel episode is very suggestive on our pathway of dialogue. Careful listening to others is essential, indeed, we might say, is the only necessary thing. The analogy is not contrived or forced. Quite the contrary. The other is for me an indication of messages that God himself wants to communicate to me in history. Attentive listening to the other's voice, discernment of the other's word, lead us not only to understand each other better, but to deepen our own approach to the divine. In general, before each neighbor, active listening is the only necessary attitude, generating space for the relationship and for understanding.

Its application to the Jewish-Christian dialogue needs no further explanation. Listening is the fundamental commitment in any attempt at dialogue, at getting close to the other, especially the one who is different. Could it be otherwise? A caring, deep and active listening, like Mary's to Jesus, is a demonstration of love as well as of intelligence. If we don't listen, we won't understand and if we don't understand who and where the others are, what's their story, their expectations, we will never be able to get close to them and show them our willingness to build bridges and strengthen ties. Without listening to the others, no dialogue is possible. That's why listening is "the better part," which will not be taken from us.

Two passages from the Psalms, a book shared by Jews and Christians

The choice of the following verses of Psalms is symbolic. Both religious traditions pray with them, often without knowing that we share these texts. A verse of Psalm 17 puts forward a definition of listening that we identify with.

> I call upon you; answer me, O God.
> Turn your ear to me; hear my speech.
> Tehillim-Psalm 17:6

Thus the Psalmist defines the relationship with God: a relationship of two wills made up by word and by listening. I invoke. You hear me. I call you. You answer me. I need you. You are there. I am encouraged to engage in dialogue because I know that my word will be accepted.

The formulation of the biblical poet is interesting: I have called upon you because you will answer me. The conversation is born in a previous dimension: the trust in the presence and the listening of the other. The believer turns to God knowing that he will get an answer. The presence of the other is the guarantee. I dare speak — the text seems to indicate — because I know there is someone in front of me that is ready to listen. Listening, then, is the space for the word. An attitude of listening is what enables the dialogue to take place. And for that there needs to be one who speaks and one who is present, in silence, a silence filled with meaning, responsive, loving and humble. Silence and word become one at the time of dialogue: silence is like the home of the word. Whoever speaks is great and whoever listens is equally great.

Many times, in interreligious dialogue programs, and in everyday dialogues as well, words are used to cite quotations from publications and to present theories. Perhaps a pedagogy of dialogue could fertilize the soil with the nutrients of listening. Because we learn to listen; it is not an innate capacity of any person. Making room for the other is something that is taught. Only when listening is strengthened are the words that emerge most likely the ones that will build a bond, and not only abstract concepts.

First, God will turn his ear. How daring the psalmist! To expect God to turn. However, just as a mirror shows us an image of our likeness, we are being taught how to listen. Inclining, leaning to listen to your neighbor, is not an act of subjugation but of love; to be able to say "I want to reach out to you," "I want to get involved," "I want to be part of what you're going to say." If we can ask God to turn his ear, metaphorically, so that we can talk, why is it so difficult here on earth to give signals to our neighbors that we are interested in what they have to say?

Listening as welcome

Finally, we chose a passage from Psalm 6, which gives us a poetic and spiritual way to understand the importance of listening.

> "The Lord has heard my plea. The Lord will receive my prayer."   Tehillim-Psalm 6:10

The psalm explains it beautifully. Listening is synonymous with receiving. Biblical poetry, especially in the book of Psalms, develops a literary figure called chiasm, in this case, a synonymic chiasm, that is, repeating an idea with different words. The meaning that the poet gives to his verses is understood in the repetition. Here in Psalm 6 we find how the word listening is interpreted:

> The Lord heard my plea,
> The Lord will **receive** my prayer.

`It is quite moving to see the verb "to listen" understood as welcoming and accepting. I listen to you, brother or sister, and, in this listening, I welcome and receive you, just by the wordless gesture of making room for you in me. Every time I'm ready to listen to you, I make room in my existence to give you a place within me. Listening is an essential prerequisite to receive integrally the other.

What do we mean by receiving? It is an exercise in self-contraction in order to make room for the others to enter, with all their being, unconditionally. Although there are aspects that we may not understand at first, we will never have access to them unless we welcome the others. To receive the others is a necessary condition in order to understand them.

In most conversations, one speaks and the other listens, and then the latter speaks and the first listens. It is an everyday, dynamic act. However, when we speak

71

of listening, we mean receptive listening, listening that, in itself, is a message. Because dialogue has a higher purpose than the mere exchange of opinions: we aim at self-change, at growing as persons, at saying words that overcome differences, at having committed attitudes of listening.

Many might think that we belittle ourselves when we make room for the others. Whether consciously or not, this is generally what we think happens. If we listen "too much" to the other, we believe that we will be losing our place. Instead, the space of listening is a generous space that makes us grow and thus it's essential to build it. It does not happen spontaneously, it requires awareness and a courageous stand. When "I listen to you," "I receive you." I'm caring and valuing your words and your being. And for that, we have to meet and get acquainted, since we don't care for what we don't love, and we don't love what we don't know.

Certainly we cannot demand love of neighbor, but we can do much to promote knowledge and mutual respect. The first step is listening, so we'll learn to care for one another. And brotherly love will be born from caring.

Times for listening

Listening is not a magic act that happens simply and spontaneously. It requires preparation and devotion. That is why we say that time and space are indispensable when it comes to listening. The experience of listening is fruitful when it takes place in the time and the space especially dedicated to it. A few of these times and spaces are sought (a dialogue meeting, an academic encounter), others are spontaneous but are equally serious and important. We need time to listen to others, especially those whom we know are more difficult to understand, those with a religious or cultural experience different from ours. Time is required so that the plant of listening may grow, mature, and acquire strength and sensitivity.

The more time we devote to discover the reflection of the other, the more we discover ourselves. They need to be moments without pressure, accompanied by the desire to be transformed. At the same time, we ought to sustain these moments throughout life. Sporadic meetings, ad hoc seminars, although very important, are not enough. For communion to happen, we must involve ourselves with the others and create reasons to get back together.

We believe that listening is refined by the experience that time gives us. The moments in common, with their accomplishments, mistakes, and unpredictable vicissitudes will be the best teachers and the best book to learn how to dialogue.

Spaces for listening

In addition to time, we need adequate spaces for the others to feel they are being heard. As we said before, they are not only formal or institutional spaces or suitable physical locations. Most importantly, they ought to be spaces that open inside ourselves or that are created around listening. Both a casual meeting and a formal event can become "spaces for listening." It depends on the attitude of the people involved; it'll require receiving the others in a friendly place and making them feel at home. And for this, we must prepare.

Remote preparation

First, we prepare for listening remotely because in order to listen properly, we must know something of the language of the other, their identity, the way they think and talk. We have to understand their language—it seems like a basic fact—but also some of their culture and their religious experience to adapt our listening and our talk—even our questions—to them. How can we listen to a Jew if we don't have any knowledge about the way he or she lives and feels? How can we listen to

Christians, if we do not understand minimally what they are telling us about their faith and actions?

This "remote" preparation to listen requires training. Training regarding the intellectual knowledge of what is important to the others, their identity, but also of their sensitivity, what makes them happy, what makes them suffer.

Proximate preparation

Proximate preparation regards the environment where the listening takes place as well as the attitude of the listener. Trying to clear our minds of prejudices favoring our most noble ideas allows us to listen "disarmed," without defenses that filter what the others say and that make us unable to understand "their" special and unique experience.

Then, in a second step, once we make sure we have listened to what has been said, the time of the evaluation and discernment, of sorting out and analysis, will come. Whoever tunes the ear to the frequency of the other has already been prepared. They have spent time listening and have been trained to listen. They have spent time preparing the necessary inner silence for the others to express themselves, and have been sufficiently informed to understand the others' language and way to grasp reality and express it.

It is a process that will always be incomplete and will require more listening and more preparation in order to move forward. It is a sort of a spiral where we begin to listen and learn about the others and the more we learn, the wider our listening is, and the more the others feel they have been heard and understood.

We can't enter the field of dialogue hastily and impatiently with the intention of obtaining immediate results. Listening alone will not guarantee the dialogue, but a committed listener is a prerequisite for dialogue to start.

Mature and sensitive listening

In trying to qualify the type of listening that dialogue requires, we wanted to add an adjective to describe it better. We like to speak of "mature listening" and "sensitive listening."

Why have we chosen these two adjectives? Neither maturity nor sensitivity can be imposed. What is then the value of characterizing as "mature" and "sensitive" the necessary listening to engage in dialogue? Whoever doesn't think of themselves as mature or sensitive, must they think that they can't dialogue?

These terms, as any other, are subject to the most varied interpretations. For "sensitive listening" we mean listening that tries to remove all preconceptions. A listening stripped of prejudice, which requires inner emptiness and, at the same time, respect and training. It is essential to try to know the references, values, and cultural and religious categories that form the others' life and personal and communitarian experience. Sensitive, trained, respectful listening must contain elements that promote understanding, a true understanding of the other.

Listening in this way may easily be considered as "mature." Listening matures and grows like human life, to the extent that it is "lived" continuously through the time and the space dedicated to it. It is mature listening because it is not false listening since it forsakes any childish desire to occupy the others' place and dominate them. Mature listening includes the poise of knowing that one exists with the other, that there is room for everyone and that everyone is important in our coexistence. It requires the patience to wait for the process and it's not attached to the results. It assesses wisely the path that one is travelling on. As Frank Whaling reminds us, "Knowing the others' religion means something more than being informed about their religious tradition. It involves finding out what makes them tick, walking in

their shoes, and seeing the world in some way through
their eyes, asking the questions that they ask."[3]

Listening is a key commitment in dialogue. Listening in order to get close to the others; listening in order
to understand; listening in order to speak and make ourselves known to the others.

A toolbox

Many times, little details like taking into account the
food that the others can eat according to their tradition,
can eliminate countless obstacles. That's why we recommend, where possible:

To open our houses and our communities; to be hos-
pitable and generous with the others; to inform each other about the calendar of our celebrations; to invite one
another to our sacred moments. Sharing a festive meal
or some other event beyond the strictly religious, which
is relevant to the lives of people, can also smooth over
obstacles inherited from thousands of years ago.

When the space provides a sense of security and the
others are comfortable, listening has a chance to take
place. It even becomes easier to control our defense
mechanisms, which sometimes urge us to avoid stressful
moments.

3.   Whaling, Frank, *Christian Theology and World Religions. A Global Approach*, London, 1986, pp. 130–131.

Chapter 5

The Art of the Word

In unison: Francisco *and* Silvina

EVERYONE HAS SOMETHING TO say and much to learn from the other. When we talk about a dialogue that goes beyond our everyday conversation and emerges from something more deeply-rooted but even of the "nullification" of the other, words become a highly sensitive area.

We were created by God and the first act that we performed, as humans, was to name what we had in front of us. Each name created for us a reality. Each concept defined and defines a universe.

Our experiences are made from language, and it is through it that we give meaning to our existence. It would be almost impossible to think of ourselves as humans without the word, which is the means by which we bond with the other. Every time we speak, we are somehow introducing ourselves, because we are committed, consciously or unconsciously, to what we express and, in turn, we give a place to the listener before us, physically or virtually.

In short, our speaking produces effects and changes in the environment in which we live. Even though we may not want it that way, it happens. And in the area of interfaith dialogue, the word neutral,—we dare say—doesn't exist, because every message has an intention, a direction at which it's aimed. It is hard to imagine the field of interreligious dialogue with surgical asepsis, as a mathematical theorem or a laboratory test. Because when we speak or are spoken to, our stories, beliefs, past wounds, come into play. So this book is an account of our explorations, since there are no foolproof formulas, but continuing learning that is incorporated into a plot being built by each one of us.

Belonging to a religious tradition is a particular phenomenon. When there is dialogue, we have the feeling that both the speaker and the listener represent in that moment their communities as well as the generations that preceded them. We are one and all at once. And it doesn't matter whether we observe and practice our religious rituals or even the strength of our faith: when someone addresses the group to which we belong, there are neither nuances nor doubts, we are all.

These comments are not meant to frighten our readers but on the contrary, we think that as porcelain and glass are as beautiful as they are fragile, interreligious dialogue is as wonderful as it is sensitive, and the more we care for it, the more encouraging will be the results.

Intellectual honesty—spiritual honesty

We have learned many of the concepts that we are sharing with you from our past life experiences; and since dialogue is a dimension of life, we are compelled to tell stories and experiences that, although personal, may help many to identify with them. Here are two stories from our lives that might deepen our subject of words and speech:

> At a symposium of Jewish-Christian dialogue, an issue was raised that in the history of both religious traditions had generated much strain: the place of Abraham as the founding father of the Jewish and/or Christian traditions. It was interesting to see how the two presenters took different paths. One introduced the topic in a scholarly way, after having made a laborious tour of the sources that illustrated and

substantiated why Abraham was the founder of their tradition.

The other person, while researching the issue from his angle, had also found sources and developments showing that Abraham was the chosen person to begin their religious tradition, but decided not to mention them despite the risk of appearing in front of the audience as less knowledgeable. The scholar did this because he perceived that these sources could hurt the feelings of those in the audience who did not belong to his flock.

What happened was very interesting because the discussion ended up not focusing on the contents of the talks presented, but on how we select what we know, how we handle the truth and our sensitivity, in order to nourish, enrich and learn without alienating others.

Reported by Silvina

In a dialogue meeting, I met the representative of a religious institution who had only recently started to participate. This person wanted to express the reasons that brought him to the meeting. In his opinion, "events such as this generate a space where no one feels discriminated against and everyone learns how not to discriminate." His position was really shareable, but it left me wanting more. It seemed to me that we could not use dialogue to build a protective "wrapper" against prejudice and discrimination.

How could I share my opinion without belittling or hurting him? Could I impose on him other goals different from the ones he had set for himself? Was it necessary to make my thinking explicit? We started a conversation. Both of us chose carefully our expressions and our arguments in order to express clearly our personal thoughts. I demanded from myself, yes, a lot of attention and interior openness to understand and make myself understood.

Reported by Francisco

From these experiences we have understood that there are two types of honesty: intellectual and spiritual. According to our experience, mentors of intellectual honesty uphold the value of impartiality in the treatment of the issues and the data which is being used: we must not deny data or withhold evidence. Honesty demands the truth, and this is the shared code by which academic communities and faculties grow and develop. However, in the name of honesty "to the letter," some mistakes have been made, because we don't always consider the sensitivity of our dialogue partner when it comes to selecting concepts or the way to explain them.

Unlike the formal framework in which academic rigor speaks of the seriousness of the presenter, interreligious dialogue is embodied in the daily lives of people. That's why the contents, in addition to being respectable and reliable, must contribute to friendship and mutual acceptance. We cannot rely exclusively on the authority of the sources, because every word, every assertion or text was said and written in different historical and "sensitive" contexts. These contexts must be taken into account and should be explained in a clear and profound way, without taking them for granted, to ensure an adequate understanding of the source (legitimate or even essential for who is using it) to which reference is made.

We also speak of "sensitive contexts" because every epoch has its own set of values, scientific paradigms, ambiguities, beliefs and sensibilities. What is written and said is always in response to a conversation that is unfolding, a reaction to the surrounding situation. The sensitivity unfolds in perceptions, comforts or discomforts, in passion or rejection—areas that are not always taken into account in the scholarly world of knowledge.

Knowledge is certainly obligatory in order to approach the others. Knowing our own identity and better yet, some acquaintance with the world of the others, which allows a minimum of understanding about their beliefs and experiences, is necessary.

So how do we realize that we are using knowledge as a constructive tool for dialogue? We humbly believe that intellectual honesty must be in harmony with what we call spiritual honesty.

When we weigh in with spiritual honesty and allow the spirit to intervene in our knowledge and ideas, true dialogue occurs. Every time we decide not to say everything (because not everything helps), even though we read it in official documents or heard it from important people, we are selecting, from among all we know, what may be good at the time, what the others can understand in its proper perspective, what can help us get close to one another. In this way, we give a real contribution to the building of a common space. The knowledge that we want to transmit about our religious identity cannot become hurtful interruptions or sterile questioning, but it must promote a gradual approach to our most authentic religious experience and sensitivity. It is a process that does not distort our faith and reality, but grows in depth thanks to the correct use of language. Paraphrasing the Christian philosopher Thomas Aquinas (1225–1274), "the when, how and where" of something that's being said is important.

Among words and meanings

Because history, myth, and scriptures are ultimately linguistic constructions produced in certain temporal contexts, meanings change as time progresses. And with this we mean that we will need to abandon the arrogant certainty that what we are saying now is exactly what our ancestors meant. No. It is our current way to understand what was said or written then. We are, as George Steiner said in *After Babel,*[1] translators, interpreters of the letter which we have inherited, and we will never fully recover the original meaning of the text because we are not them and we do not live in the coordinates of their time.

1. Steiner, George, *Después de Babel. Aspectos del lenguaje y la traducción*, México, Fondo de Cultura Económica, 2013

In the experience we gave before, we saw how two different lecturers appeared dissonant in front of their audience. One, with the rigor of the researcher, laid on the table contents and sources relevant to the subject. But what happened is that in this speech, the lecturer's own view of reality did not emerge. And we feel that this is what interfaith dialogue is claiming in this instance: that we get involved, that we quote the sources and later on speak with our own voice, toward a goal that will allow us to encounter one another.

We are not the Jews of Jesus' day, nor the Christians of the Crusades, nor the Tannaites and the Amoraim[2] or the authorities of the Inquisition. We are who we are today, with our names, faces, stories, fears, with the words that we like, and with the concepts that hurt. We may use citations from different moments in history, but let's be careful in our selection of them so that they can fulfill the task we are proposing: to walk together, side by side, enjoying the richness of diversity.

Ortega y Gasset wrote: "when we converse, we live within a society; when we think we remain alone." Thus, we invite you to begin together a conversation by using an interesting method: the art of asking.

In two voices: Silvina

The art of asking

I must confess that the path of dialogue is challenging, touching and often thankless. The intentions of two persons who are facing each other are not always the same, although both may describe that act as dialogue.

2. *Tannaites* is a term used to designate the Rabbinic sages whose interpretations were recorded in the Mishnah, between 30 and 200 CE. They are the writers of the Mishnah, an exegetical body of compiled Jewish law, which collects and consolidates the Jewish oral tradition developed from the times of the Torah or written law until its codification by Rabbi Yehudah Hanasi towards the end of the second century. *Amoraites* is the name by which are collectively known the Jewish sages of the diaspora who produced the Gemara. The Gemara and the Mishnah together form the Talmud. The Mishnah is the basic text and the Gemara comprises commentary on and analysis of the Mishnah, in order to complete it.

I have learned that the will is important but not enough. Or rather, each will expresses a different desire, which not always intersects with the other's. One of the most interesting challenges is to learn how to ask: to ask ourselves and those whom we are educating. Not everything that has a question mark is a question. I intend to share with you short stories of my life in the area of dialogue, in order to extract the core of the teaching that I obtained from each of them.

Teaching how to ask

At an annual meeting I conduct in my community Bet-El between children in Bar Mitzvah preparation and students of catechesis and confirmation of the church of San Patricio, we encourage the kids to ask questions. On this occasion the atmosphere of the meeting was of frank camaraderie. I was surprised at how many parents were present: at times, there are more adults than children. And I don't really know whether they come to share the joy of the experience or to visit a Jewish community for the first time or "to check" what will happen in those two hours.

Anyway, returning to this gathering, one of them, Jewish, asks the Christians: How can you believe that a virgin had a son? At that moment, my blood ran cold. Not so much because of the genuine question of someone who was not trained in the faith of the miracle of the nativity, but because I, an adult, had not taken the time to teach this person how to ask. Because asking, in interreligious dialogue, is not a free ride without any limitations, at least, not in the first instance.

From that moment on, I taught my students some principles with regards to asking questions in the context of interfaith dialogue:

> a) Beliefs cannot be questioned. These are not questions looking for information, but judgments disguised as questions. Christians believe in the Virgin and an answer to that question contributes nothing to

the dialogue. Because the answer involves faith, and faith is not explained, but it's felt, perceived, borne. Similarly, the Jews would have no rational answers to questions such as the parting of the Sea of Reeds after leaving Egypt, an event that can' be explained only in terms of faith in the power of God.

b) Speaking the same language does not mean we understand each other. We ask and answer according to the paradigm of values and terms we have learned through our education. I'm going to take a very common example, especially in the dialogue among children. Jewish kids often ask about the meaning of communion, to which question a confirmation student responded: We receive the body and blood of Christ.

I cannot describe in words the faces of the Jewish children. Imagine what it means for someone who has not been educated in the Christian faith to hear that there is a ritual in which someone's flesh and blood is received. There, I understood again the fundamental role of educators: to intervene in that interface where two are speaking the same language but the words do not mean the same.

So I took the liberty to include myself in the dialogue and I asked my colleagues, the catechists, to explain what it meant to receive the body and blood in plain words, because for us, Jews, bread and wine are simply symbols of sustenance and joy, respectively. It was then that the group of Christians reflected on how many times we take things for granted when the others, in addition to not understanding us, may be put off because the interpretation of what is being said turns out to be less than friendly. How do you dialogue with someone who celebrates taking someone's blood?

c) Ask in order to know, not to provoke the speaker in front of the audience.

Once I was invited to give a talk, together with a priest, to students in a Catechetical Seminary. I was very happy to speak to educators, because that's where I think change will happen, not in the context of the great international symposiums exclusively.

The priest and I explained the commonalities and the differences between the Jewish and the Christian Passover, the Shavuot and Pentecost. Afterwards, I had the opportunity to share some of my experiences of interreligious dialogue. During the time for questions, a student asked me:

Why don't you believe in Jesus Christ?

Several ideas crossed my mind in an instant, but fundamentally, I had a feeling of discomfort. I did not like something about that situation. Everyone's expectant and silent gaze was upon me. There was a sense of "victory" in the eyes of the questioner. Didn't she know what caused the schism between some Jews and others, who later on, became Christians? Was she unaware that for two thousand years the Jews were persecuted, attacked, forcibly converted and massacred for not accepting the messiahship of Jesus? What should I answer? In the end, I decided to be honest rather than politically correct:

> This question doesn't do any good to anybody, especially in this situation. Do you expect me to say here that Jesus is not the Messiah? Do you intend, with that apparently harmless question, to make me say something that will draw us apart again, and diminish the climate of fellowship that we had achieved? Is the issue between Jews and Christians why one group did not stay with the other's faith or rather, how can we decide, once and for all, to accept each other as legitimately different with equal rights? An awkward silence followed, and then the audience burst into a liberating applause. We had learned not to slap with the question, but to use the precious little time to be together and to build fraternity.

d) Giving up the illusion of the conversion:

When we sit down at a meeting of dialogue, as Jews or Christians, the last thing we expect to hear is the question: what do you lack yet in order for you to convert? Dialogue is precisely the contrary. It's to leave the "ring" without sizing up any longer our strength, but finding potential in our differences. How can I answer that question? And what would it bring to the encounter between two? The encounter between two is none other than that, encounter and two. There is nothing more foolish than pretending to ask why I don't stop being who I am in order to be like the other. Such interventions, in my case, call for silence.

In short, we ask in order to get closer, to learn more, to know the others, to get rid of prejudices, to tell the others that they matter to us, to unravel aspects of the others that we find difficult to understand. We ask in order to grow, each in our interior, hoping to grow in the others and with the others. We ask because the knowledge of others never ends, for they are beings created by Him, infinite, and as such infinite, rich, creative, container and content. There are so many beautiful questions that we could ask, still, why do we insist on questions that drive us into the abyss, hurt us, disrespectfully provoke us, separate us and do not leave us wanting to use again our limited time if the result is suffering or shame?

Lessons along the way

We want to share what happened at this point of the book. We had decided that the topic "the art of asking" was going to be written in unison, because we did not have conflicting opinions. Silvina had already written some reflections, which she gave to Francisco, so that he could add his examples and ideas and thus compose together a single text. Francisco received what had been written and decided that it should remain as it was, without additions or modifications, because it also expressed his thoughts completely.

Instead, he wrote his own comments and reflections on what Silvina wrote. That text appears at the end of this account.

The interesting thing is the message in this gesture of Francisco's, is one more piece in this pedagogy of dialogue. At times, the other's word is so valid and the bond so strong that it is not necessary to force any contribution or intervention with the only purpose of not being "left out." Sometimes excess words, overlapping ideas or unnecessary comments are subtle ways of sizing up against the other; "to have the last word" is a resource by those who, pretending to show they love dialogue, want to win an imaginary contest. So, what you will now read are Francisco's reflections on the text of Silvina. It is one way to demonstrate that well-understood dialogue completes us and makes us beautiful.

In two voices: Francisco

The art of asking: a necessary education

We learn to ask. Silvina's text is eloquent and provides valuable lessons, which are useful to us Christians as well, when it comes to asking about the religious tradition of others and answering questions about our faith or religious experience.

Ours are not the innocent questions of children who discover the world for the first time. Our questions, by young people or adults, are already conditioned by what we have learned and mislearned about the others. Most of the time, they are loaded with superficial, partial or totally misunderstanding of the others. Other times, as Silvina explains very well, they don't have an upright intention: they only try to "expose" the others in front of an audience or our own selves, and challenge them on key issues for their lives, which are difficult (if not impossible) to explain to those who do not share their faith and their experience.

In several meetings with Christian kids, most of whom had a great openness and sensitivity to interfaith dialogue or to dialogue in general, I noticed questions full of good intentions to know the others' lives, and a sincere interest in getting close to them. However, they concealed a great number of prejudices and stereotypes. They were questions which would have literally hurt or separated rather than united, had they not been put in the proper context or to the right people.

To ask a Jew: "Why do you all have a lot of money?" or "Why are you so interested in controlling the mass media?" certainly reveals false perceptions of reality. They are a low blow to the person questioned and an additional manifestation of ingrained prejudices as a consequence of the history and tragedy of Jewish-Christian relations.

So, do we have to censor the questions and make a list of things that can and cannot be asked? Is it prudent not to ask anything to avoid misunderstandings, errors, misinterpretations? Is it possible to learn about the other and get rid of the prejudices that I maintain, even those of which I'm not fully aware, if I cannot ask the others anything?

The question and trust

Let's go step by step. The art of asking requires, first of all, the context of trust and listening of which we have talked at length in these pages. We cannot ask questions that we know beforehand will stir up hard feelings or bring positions into question, if an appropriate bond of trust has not been established. This also applies if we have not listened to the others, giving them the opportunity to express what they deem appropriate about themselves, and giving us the opportunity to follow their expressions in an unprejudiced way, with the honest intention to understand them.

To be formed in order to ask

Asking properly is an art for which we must be formed. The training must start by personally knowing those others, sharing something of their lives, reading or even studying valuable materials dealing with their religious experience. It implies that we open our minds and hearts to matters of their faith that may go beyond our personal understanding or mental picture of what faith and religion are.

In order to know how to ask, we must have an experience—even if small—of the others, know something (it will never be all) of their interests and language. We ought to consider and gradually deepen our knowledge of their codes and ways of living. After acquiring this patrimony, we can then express what we want to know more about the others, deepening their reality, not without having taken into account the suggestions wisely put forward by Silvina.

Asking is not synonymous with polemicizing

The art of asking requires also that we abandon the spirit of controversial contention, which we slyly have, often times, against the others. At times, we consider them "equal" to us, being puzzled by their diversity, and then we move on trying to assimilate them to our understandings of reality or to fight them with questions and hurtful responses. Other times we consider them so "different" that we don't even deign to ask something substantial because we think we will never understand and get closer to one another.

In order to ask correctly, we have to know that the others are equal to us (in humanity, dignity) and different (in religious tradition, history and life experience) at the same time. We can get to know them because we have a lot in common, but we must also learn from them because we are different. The ultimate intention of our asking is to get to know them and get close to them, establishing a bond that will help us grow by better understanding the others and ourselves in our respective identities and our common humanity.

In two voices: Silvina

The answer as ethics

I had the opportunity to share, together with a priest, a Judeo-Christian round table, to talk about values and leadership, during a national meeting of business leaders. What a difficult task I had been asked! While researching these values, I realized that they had much to do with the way we are moving along here, that is, our examination of words, ideas and actions for interreligious dialogue.

One of the concepts that I would like to share is that dialogue summons us to an ethic of responsibility. It is interesting, because the word "responsibility," from the Latin *responsum*, speaks of the ability to respond. While the Hebrew equivalent of the word "response" is *teshuva*, which refers to the concept of introspection and reflection that we do on the Ten Days of Repentance, which begin with the Jewish New Year (Rosh Hashanah) and end with the Day of Atonement (Yom Kippur), the holiest day of the year. So, while one root of this word invites us to give answers, in Hebrew, responsibility abides in the capacity of questioning oneself.

Maybe that's why questions and answers, especially on issues of interreligious dialogue, have to do with taking responsibility for what we ask and what we say. Then, when we speak about responsibility, we presuppose an "ethic," because when we make a commitment to the others, we bring into play the natural ethical obligation towards them, which we would have before any other human being who was next to us.

A way to develop that "ethic" is being aware of our responsibility in our questions and our answers, because our acts have value by virtue of the consequences that they provoke. What we do, what we say, where we participate and where we don't, leaves a mark. Let's be responsible with the traces that we leave. Let's be ethically responsible for our words and our actions. A sincere dialogue must necessarily be ethically responsible.

Responsibility and freedom

Hans Jonas, one of the leaders in the field of applied ethics, points out something that I think is wonderful: responsibility is the burden of freedom, that is, responsibility emanates from freedom; it is a must for anyone who experiences what it means to be free, and I dare say, for whoever wishes to be free.

How much I like to think of the concept of responsibility not so much as a burden but as a dimension that comes from my own freedom!

The renowned Viennese psychiatrist Victor Frankel, founder of the school of logotherapy, liked to say that "freedom is in danger of degenerating into mere arbitrariness unless we live it in terms of responsibleness. That is why I recommend that the Statue of Liberty on the East Coast be supplemented by a Statue of Responsibility on the West Coast."[3] Both concepts, freedom and responsibility do not exist without each other. Freedom creates responsibility and responsibility allows me to be free. And what's this book but an experience of absolute freedom and absolute responsibility, because of the beliefs of each one and the profound respect for the other's?

I love etymologies and my strong suit is Hebrew.

In Hebrew, the word "responsibility" is *ahrayut*—a very interesting word, if any! We find in this term first the word *ah*— "brother." Responsibility is put to the test when there is fraternal awareness. And it doesn't refer exclusively to affective relationships, but it applies to any relationship with our neighbor, who is not a stranger, but a brother and sister, another with whom we share a bond.

---

3.   Frankl, Victor. *Man's Search for Meaning*, Boston, Beacon Press, 2006.

The concept of responsibility develops in this awareness, in recognizing the existence of the others to whom
I owe my attitudes, because we do have a relationship.

On the other hand, and according to this sense of fraternity, the word *ahrayut* includes in its written form the
word *aher*—the other. And here I'm reminded of Levi-
nas, when he declares that the other is what I myself
am not, what is anterior to me and thanks to whom, I
insist, thanks to whom, I am who I am. The relationship
with another is not cognitive, but purely ethical. I am in
function with the others, and, therefore, in order to be
sincere when we speak of ethical behavior, the commitment to them is essential. Ethics begins in the otherness
of the others and in the interaction with them.

Questions and answers invite us to a profound, at
times painful, reflection on what we say, how we think
of others, how prejudices are sometimes invisible. We
learn to ask as well as to answer.

In unison: Francisco *and* Silvina

Responsibility for the words

> "Languages are not only 'used,' they are not only
> principles of communication, personal expression or
> collective use: they contain the experience of peoples
> and they transmit it, but only to the extent we are
> willing to recognize their ability to speak to us."[4]

It may sound like a truism, but we want to emphasize the vital importance of language when it comes to
speaking. Many speak of the "uses of language" and
condense in that term a relationship with words that
separates them from their profound meaning and their
mnemonic traces. Speaking is not just a tool, language is
not just "used" as a mere vehicle, operational and func-
tional; the words which we use define us.

---

4. Bordelois, Ivonne, *La palabra amenazada*, Buenos Aires, Libros del
   Zorzal, 2005.

Bordelois illustrates this topic with something very interesting: "In Latin 'I have spoken' is said *locutus sum,* which morphologically means 'I have been spoken to.'"

When we speak, we present ourselves. Language is interwoven with the meanings and images that spring from our words. By this we mean that to speak, for us, is an act of responsibility, toward us and toward our neighbors, because what comes out of us can be the strongest bridge or the cruelest thuggery.

Throughout our lives we have learned words that caress and words that separate. We have understood that thinking before speaking, and examining what we receive from others before repeating it, are conscious acts that contribute to situations of encounter.

The very writing of this book involves a careful and sensitive effort with regard to the words that we use, because we want to share what we have without hurting others and without putting you, our readers aside.

We consult each other and review our sources. When speaking of ourselves and of the other, we try to put ourselves in the place of the other. We go over the painful events of our past from a historic but also linguistic perspective: which words could have been used to avoid causing these wounds, which concepts and attitudes regarding ideas and their formulation could have attenuated the impact of so much trouble.

The following story happened during the writing of this book. It illustrates what we mean when we speak of the significant weight of words and what we say about the others, not only in content but in form. It further shows the implications of certain expressions, rooted in our discourse about others, often without any reflection upon them, expressions that accumulate and have a kind of snowball effect on those who receive them. It points to a feeling of frustration that these "pseudo-truths" will not be eradicated, and then the real encounter between Jews and Christians will happen but with great difficulty in all of its dimensions.

I went on a trip by bus with the youth movement in my community, to a life education camp for three weeks in the city of Tandil, in the province of Buenos Aires. As a chaperon, I always sit in the companion seat and bring the Torah scroll with me. The driver, who was sitting across the aisle, asked me what I was carrying and I answered that it was the Torah scroll containing the first five books of the Bible. I also mentioned, in my "dialogical" spirit, that Jesus would have read from a similar scroll when he went to the synagogue, as recounted by the Gospel.

He took a moment, looked me in the eyes and said: "What do you feel about being the ones who killed Christ. How can you still live with the fact that you crucified God?"

The first feeling was a chill in my soul, followed by my being perplexed. Again, I was back to square one, having to explain once again what persists in the knowledge and discourses of many!

Again, I was looked at with scorn by someone absolutely convinced of my responsibility for the death of Christ! And the conversation went on: "The film shows very clearly how you killed him! He came to redeem you, the chosen people, and you killed him!" Each "you" of this good man was, for me, a slap. I tried to explain. I asked him to speak to his parish priest and ask what he thought of this (maybe he could share with him what the Declaration *Nostra Aetate* of Vatican II says); and that movies sometimes do things to attract scandal. Well, I don't think I made it: a short chat could not possibly counteract years of an idea fixed with iron nails in his mind and transmitted over the centuries in the genetic memory of many. I decided not to pursue the matter and offered him a bottle of water, which he gladly accepted.

Recounted by Silvina

In two voices: Francisco

Responsibility for the words of others

"Locutus sum," Silvina reminds us in the preceding paragraphs, means in its morphology *"I have been spoken to."* Have we Christians been "spoken to" in the story recounted by Silvina, in the poorly phrased words of the bus driver?

It is a question that really challenges us. For our words, always and necessarily, involve others. In addition to responsibility for the words we speak, we acquire responsibility for the words that others say about our group, our institution, our religion.

What could we say to a Jewish friend who listens to similar statements and may not have Silvina's training, judgment and capacity for dialogue?

These are very difficult questions to answer. But this book we are writing together attempts to address them. What do we, Christians, say to Christians who express themselves in that way? Can we or do we have to take responsibility for their words?

Clearly, Silvina's story confronts us with a very entrenched reality: socially preconceived ideas born out of layers and overlapping layers of misunderstandings and prejudices. In spite of changing attitudes and the efforts by churches, the Catholic Church in particular, to knock down myths and issue documents, there is a "snowball effect" that continues to haunt us. Where did the bus driver get his ideas from? Did he conceive of them himself? It is very likely that he didn't.

He heard them when he was little in his family, around the neighborhood, perhaps even in the parish or the temple, or he may have heard them on TV or the cinema. He is saturated with these ideas in such a way that he doesn't question them. They have become "truths," which he doesn't need to reconsider. They are so, period. Silvina reminded us of the axioms that conform our thinking and that we face day after day.

95

The Second Vatican Council in its Declaration *Nostra Aetate* (4), on the relations of the Church to non-Christian religions says:

> True, the Jewish authorities and those who followed their lead pressed for the death of Christ; still, what happened in His passion cannot be charged against all the Jews, without distinction, then alive, nor against the Jews of today. All should see to it, then, that in catechetical work or in the preaching of the word of God they do not teach anything that does not conform to the truth of the Gospel and the spirit of Christ.... The Church...decries hatred, persecutions, displays of anti-Semitism, directed against Jews at any time and by anyone.

Subsequent post-conciliar documents take up again this idea and bring it ahead,[5] to the point of condemning anti-Semitism as a true sin.

Looking at these texts that form the true thought of the Catholic Church towards the Jews and Judaism, can any Catholic continue to support ideas such as those of the bus driver? Obviously not! What is our responsibility, as Christian educators, for the words that "Christians in the street" use, which speak for us all?

First of all, it is a huge responsibility: as educators, our words must lead to the building of new paradigms of understanding and language, appropriate to reality and the thought of the Church.

Here is a personal account.

---

5. "Information concerning these questions is important at all levels of Christian instruction and education. Among sources of information, special attention should be paid to the following: –catechisms and religious textbooks; –history books; –the mass-media (press, radio, cinema, television). The effective use of these means presupposes the thorough formation of instructors and educators in training schools, seminaries and universities." From the *Guidelines and Suggestions for Implementing the Conciliar Declaration "Nostra Aetate" (n. 4)* (Commission for Religious Relations with the Jews). December 1, 1974; and *Notes on the Correct Way to Present the Jews and Judaism in preaching and catechesis in the Roman Catholic Church* (Commission for Religious Relations with the Jews). December 1, 1974.

Going by taxi to Silvina's Jewish school where she works, the driver asked me:

"Are you going to the Jewish center?"

"Yes," I reply.

"Are you Jewish?"

"No," I say innocently, adding "I'm working with a rabbi on a book on the pedagogy of dialogue."

The taxi driver then poured forth, in a few blocks, his entire battery of prejudices and concluded:

"It is impossible to dialogue with them."

I confess it was hard to understand what attitude to take: reject violently his words, expose his false beliefs, seek to explain some of what we do in our dialogue? Unfazed externally, I told him that my experience was very different, and I shared some personal episodes regarding our dialogue. I took a step further and tried to make him understand—using language that would not attack him directly—the falsehoods which he had said. We kept on talking for a while after the payment of the fare. I don't know if I convinced him or if I retraced with him his itinerary of prejudices. But I thought I sowed doubt about his myths about Jews and Judaism. He doubted his ideas. And that, I believe, is a first step.

Our responsibility for the words of others, especially the most hurtful, must be practiced with determination. We must return continually to the Christian thought expressed by the Council and help it to permeate all Christians, not only those better formed. As the cited documents indicate, the catechesis, the history textbooks, and the press are qualified speech (inasmuch as they educate) that must change in order to gradually transform the attitudes of Christians, as for the sake of our Jewish brothers and sisters and, above all, for the sake of ourselves.

In unison: Francisco *and* Silvina

Let's talk about what hurts

> *Once in a while*
> *one must pause*
> *to contemplate oneself*
> *without daily enjoyment*
> *examine the past*
> *section by section*
> *stage by stage*
> *tile by tile*
> *without crying out lies*
> *but singing the truths.*
>
> Mario Benedetti[6]

We decided to take a break in this book to examine, section by section, stage by stage, as the poet says, those words and concepts, which we possess, regarding others. For we have made a covenant with sincerity: we do not want to stop writing about what hurts, which persists from the remotest times. We know it is often difficult to uproot prejudice, but we trust that those who are reading this book, have the vocation to learn and review their own practices regarding these issues we are dealing with.

We said that it is complex to retrace the process by which a prejudice is formed, because by its own definition, a prejudice is an axiomatic and absolute assertion. Thus, as any axiom, it is not questioned but replicated as the basis to justify a position or attitude with regards to the others. It is an affirmation that enters the culture, gets installed in a certain group that receives it and repeats it thoughtlessly. It is difficult to disarm it with arguments because it is an opinion that cannot be discussed or verified. What a prejudice says does not accept any arguments against it because there is nothing that can be done to weaken the force of this declaration.

---

6. Inventario, poesía completa (1950–1985). Benedetti, Mario. Buenos Aires: Ed. Nueva Imagen, 1993.

And in general, its purpose is hurtful because it defines the other by a negative, stereotyped, and universal trait, inflames certain masses and often turns into violence.

Prejudice is a declaration that is characterized by generalization and certainty. When we hear that "all... are..." and a derogatory epithet appears after the verb, we are facing a biased message. And in general, those messages are carried by majority groups about certain minorities, whether they are religious, economic, social, ethnic, etc. Historically, in times of social, political or economic crises, prejudices are often used against certain minorities that are seen as the culprits of the bad times. There are political leaders who build them, spread them and use them. Prejudices are not generated spontaneously, but they are placed in circulation with the intention to manipulate people to carry and spread them, and to act upon them. Thus we find them in speeches, articles in the media, and in books.

We can deal with these very intense issues by retracing the time in history in which certain prejudices were created and the function they had at the time. Because, we insist, while we cannot fail to recognize the tracks of history on ourselves, we are not obliged to follow them if they bring us to disrespectful and unfair behavior with regard to our neighbors. We are free to decide not to circulate those false truths but to reveal their hidden meaning and then to inaugurate a new repertoire of real truths, those which, as the poet says, we can sing with total joy.

In two voices: Silvina

The return trip

The camp ended and we took a bus again to return home. Once more, I sat near the drivers. The one who was driving asked me:

"What do you Jews believe in?"

And the other chided him:

"Shut up! Do not say the word 'Jew.' That might bother her."

And looking at me, he asked me:

"Are you offended if I call you Jew?"

To which I replied:

"Absolutely not. It'd be the same if I call you Christian, would it bother you?"

And I went on:

"Anyhow, I appreciate your kindness for asking me how I prefer to be called."

My camp experience ended here. But at the same time, a new chapter opened in this adventure, trying to be aware of what we say and what we think, of ourselves and of the others, feeling free to share it with others, and joyful, as in this last story, because some of the hope I had lost on the first part of our trip, returned after our friendly conversation.

Much is learned living day by day about ourselves and about others. What happened with these work colleagues was very interesting. Surely each had different life experiences regarding Jewishness, which was manifested in our conversations. One of them had learned somehow that the word "Jew" was used as an insult, so he did not utter it lightly, but took this information and decided on its meaning: he did not want to pronounce any words which would offend me, since he didn't know me at all. And he had the tact to ask me whether his way of addressing me was correct or, instead, was causing me distress.

At that time, I could visualize a kind of an itinerary of the prejudice: A negative idea about the other starts being used. But this does not guarantee that such prejudice will flourish. When a false or hurtful idea about any neighbor spreads, everyone is free to take it or at least to question it.

And better yet would be what happened to me, for example, on that occasion: to be asked about the best way to be addressed. How interesting! Perhaps a public statement that the word "Jew" need not to be an insulting name may not be as effective as working on the sensitivity of the other, on the importance of the right words and on the need to live together and learn from each diversity.

As the conversation continued about my beliefs and practices, one of them said, "I love to learn from each person and get to know them, in order to understand how to respect them."

So simple and yet, so deep. In this way we build bonds, communities, societies, step by step, word by word, with the humility of knowing how to be in the place of the others and the freedom of not repeating uncritically everything we receive or learn.

Language is one of the strongest identifying features of any community. We believe that much of the anguish of our time is due to having abandoned language as a social amalgam, as a foundation of our growth and creativity. It has been transformed into a simple "medium," perhaps because of the power developed by the media. But words are not just empty entities, mere channels of information. Words can save us from the barely contained indifference, apathy or aggression of our times. "In truth," says Ivonne Bordelois,[7] "language is not sufficient for us but it is necessary; words alone won't save us but we can't be saved without words."

When words fail, then violence, stigma, clichés, ignorance and prejudice win. So, we invite you to consider every word as a brush on a blank canvas. We can paint the best work of art with them, but that depends only on us.

---

7.   Ibid, p. 136.

Chapter 6

About Bonds, Emotions, and Dialogue

In unison: Francisco *and* Silvina

INTERRELIGIOUS DIALOGUE BELONGS TO both the public and the private spheres. On one hand, it is a subject of discussion in international forums, in the drafting of documents and in politics. Religious leaders with broad representation decide an agenda regarding dialogue, with its steps forward and its setbacks. At the same time, experiences take place among people in the private sphere, which may not always coincide with the important postulates of the public sphere.

The private area has other codes, dialogue is lived in another way. It is complex because we are appealing to what is human within each one, those portions of our being which often remain little explored and challenged. We respond to significant public structures, such as the religious institutions to which we adhere, but we also build bonds every day that form us, we define our friends and our "enemies," those opposed to us, we decide whom to trust and whom not. In short, private life is not fully governed by the contentions of public life, and it ends up influencing it. In our own area we'll be the ones to recognize our limitations and our possibilities.

This introduction has to do with the topic we want to develop in this chapter. Because when we talk about dialogue between human beings, awareness of the role of affection and the bond in a relationship is as important as our intellectual skills.

Edgar Morin[1] said that "everything that is human involves affectivity." We are beings dependent on the affection and the connections around us. As people of faith, we know that the mystery dwells there where the intellectual analysis finds its limits. Interfaith dialogue requires also a space to think about bonds and affections, because as humans, we would not have done a complete job if we did not dive into these issues. They are spaces of daily expression of which we cannot do without, having an effect in areas increasingly more external and public.

We know that we are entering into very personal terrain, where we all have our own experiences and about which it is difficult to give recommendations. But we prefer to err rather than not try.

Interpersonal bonds, foundation for all forms of dialogue

> Dialogue cannot exist, however, in the absence of a profound love for the world and for people. The naming of the world, which is an act of creation and re-creation, is not possible if it is not infused with love. Love is at the same time the foundation of dialogue and dialogue itself. It is thus necessarily the task of responsible subjects and cannot exist in a relation of domination.... Because love is an act of courage, not of fear, love is commitment to others. No matter where the oppressed are found, the act of love is commitment to their cause.... And this commitment, because it is loving, is dialogical.
>
> *Paulo Freire[2]*

We have often wondered how it was possible to present the work we are proposing: where did the ideas that fill lines and pages come from? Where did we get the concepts that helped us recognize the elements that lead to dialogue and allow us to learn to dialogue? Our

1. Morin, Edgar. *El Método. La Humanidad de la Humanidad.* La Identidad Humana. Madrid, Cátedra, 2003, p. 135.
2. Freire, Paulo. *Pedagogy of the Oppressed,* London – New York, Continuum, 2000, p. 89.

response was almost immediate: there is a bond between us. A bond that takes us forward, helping us overcome misunderstandings and deepen the experience of the other, enabling us to convey the contents of our religious experience more effectively and to make them more understandable.

Our experience can be transferable to other people who wish to engage in Judeo-Christian understanding. This bold affirmation unravels something instilled in the type of bond of which we speak: it is not a purely emotional bond, such as the friendship between two people of different religions who know and try to understand one another. A relationship of this sort originates spontaneously, cannot be generated or created. It simply happens or it doesn't.

Instead, the bond that unites us and that contains friendship as well is more than just a spontaneous feeling. It is the result of a creative will, of the desire to generate it and of its constant, precise and determined pursuit.

Is it possible, then, from my perspective, to "create" a bond with someone different from me, with another with whom I don't share the same religion or the same work or study spaces; with whom I don't have a convergent story, built by spending time together at some level throughout the years? Is it really possible?

We think so. This type of bond is certainly possible. It is an interpersonal connection that includes the dimension of feelings such as friendship, and without being limited by their naturalness, seeks to overcome the barriers of misunderstandings and the lack of spontaneity, while being created and recreated continuously.

What could be the motivation for such a bond? In simple words: What or who makes me "love" those different from me, the others with whom I share our common human dignity but with whom I don't intersect at almost any point? I'm neither their friend nor their relative or co-religionist. What would attract me to them? Why would I go out to meet them?

In these pages, we have tried to answer, from our own experience, these apparently obvious but fundamental questions.

The Jewish-Christian dialogue emerges from personal relationships imbued with the mutual trust and listening we have spoken so much about. They also have the need for affectivity, that feeling or human value which either arises spontaneously or can be built with patience and time, and which allows us to read accurately the others' intentions, beyond their words, so that closeness and understanding may be possible.

We have tested it: the personal bond between a Jew and a Christian allows prejudices, which sometimes burst their way ruthlessly between the two religions or cultures, to be gradually overcome. Meeting one another in our common humanity tears down barriers that theological studies or institutional meetings alone cannot.

In Two voices: Silvina

Bond as message and love as responsibility

Paul Watzlawick (1921–1997) one of the principal authors of communication theory and radical constructivism defines five axioms that characterize human communication. The first is: One cannot, not communicate. Every behavior is a form of communication. Because behavior does not have a counterpart (there is no "anti-behavior") it is impossible not to communicate.

This helps us understand that any bond, even when it lacks words, is a form of communication. Many more factors than we could ever imagine are involved in a relationship, and everything can be meaningful and become a message, both for ourselves and for the others. Venturing into building relationships with the others is in itself very valuable, a wager that something can be created. It takes only our willingness to make it happen.

We develop as human beings both in the physical and symbolic worlds: everything that happens has a particular meaning for each one of us. We create our own history with the way we understand our reality, in an endless conversation between logic and empirical facts, between ideas and emotions. Our subjectivity and affectivity are an inseparable part of our lives.

Re-appreciate tenderness

Some might think that it is a rather naive position. In a globalized world where the nuances and richness of our particular stories are blurred, where little is said about tenderness, it may seem somewhat anachronistic to believe that dialogue with others occurs more easily when "we let ourselves be loved," when we allow ourselves to "feel" stripped of any mental and intellectual strategy answering to the mandates of our own making. There is a lot of content in affection, even without words. There is much subtext in a loving current between people.

It takes fertile time to build those ties, as we have said from the beginning, time to create them, nurture them and preserve them, time and willingness to unite myself to the others, with hope and without demands. When do I know that I'm really getting to know the others? When their thoughts and feelings matter to me. When I don't "parcel" the others out as if they were objects, but welcome them in their entirety.

Love of neighbor and of oneself

We belong to religious traditions that prescribe love of God, love of neighbor and love of self.

> "You shall love your neighbor as yourself, I am the Lord." (Leviticus 19:18)

> "You shall love the Lord your God with all your heart, and with all your soul, and with all your strength, and with all your mind; and your neighbor as yourself." (Luke 10:27)

"For the whole law is summed up in a single commandment, 'You shall love your neighbor as yourself.'" (Galatians 5:14)

"You do well if you really fulfill the royal law according to the scripture, 'You shall love your neighbor as yourself.'" (James 2:8)

We are prescribed to love, as if love could be ordered. It may seem that the precept is not compatible with the feeling. However, both dimensions are not contradictory but complementary in the concept of love according to the Jewish tradition. Because love is a dimension of the responsibility toward the other.

One story recounts that Rabbi Moshe Leib of Sasov[3] told his followers:

I learned what true love is from a conversation I overheard between two peasants. One asked the other, "Tell me, Ivan, my friend, do you love me?" The other replied, "Of course. I love you very much" Still dissatisfied, the first asked again: "Do you know, my friend, what makes me suffer?" Ivan, not without surprise, replied: "How can I know what makes you suffer?" "If you don't know what causes me pain, how can you say that you love me?"

Rabbi Moshe Leib, pausing to allow the meaning of the story to sink in, concluded: "Understand, my children: true love means to know and feel what causes others pain and suffering."

This story reveals what it means to love the others and to consider them neighbors. Love is the chance that we have to express our sensitivity to the needs of the person next to each of us. Love is the only way we can heal sadness, oppression, inequity. Love is the key to bringing light to the one in darkness, warmth to the one who

---

3.   Rabbi Moshe Leib was born in 1745 and died in 1807. He was rabbi in the city of Sassov, in present day Ukraine, and was known for his great capacity for love and for his acts of *Tzedakah* (social justice). They called him the "Father of widows and orphans."

shivers from loneliness, tenderness to the prisoner of his or her own alienation.

Perhaps the difference between the most prevalent concept of love and the concept of love proposed by the tradition of Israel is that the former is "possessed," while love is "dwelt in;" it is a reality that must be "produced."

There is no love without two, the lover and the beloved, and without a project between them, a real and concrete action, a lifetime commitment. It is not a simple altruistic emotion that dignifies the person. Love is the engine that guides a particular action every time I see the one next to me as neighbor, that is, as "another" that defines me and challenges me to be in the other, for the other, and for myself.

There is no Judaism in solitude. There is no chance to be observant of the Law if we cannot "observe" around us, and looking at those who are next to us, we see ourselves in them and shape and reclaim our own being.

Therefore, the mandate is twofold: "Love your neighbor as yourself." The precept calls us to transcend individuality. Love unfolds in the dimensions of humility and solidarity. Life in community is an expression of love. The commitment to be responsible for the other is a concrete witness of love.

This does not imply in any way sacrificing one's own self. It is written: "As yourself," that is, there is no true love if the level in which love is given and received is not evened out. No love justifies the immolation, the scourging, the cancellation of who I am in favor of the other, because if I cannot build myself up, I will not be able to give much to whoever is by my side, much less to the one who needs me. But on the other hand, to have one's own needs satisfied is not the end of the journey: I need that the others also access their own horizons. And taking their hand to accompany them on their own journey is called "love."

Love, thus, is a sacred act that unfolds on the stage of real life. And by loving, we recover the ability to perceive the very presence of God in us, when we are together.

We can thus understand the end of the verse, often omitted by those who cite the First and the Second Testament: "Love your neighbor as yourself. I am God."

When we love our neighbor as ourselves, then "I am God," that is, only then God will be perceived in the deepest of his manifestations. He does not do it for us. We summon him, with our acts of love, to reveal his presence. It only depends on our actions.

Affection as an opportunity

I want to think of love not as a command but as a possibility to open up to the other, a catalyst for mutual knowledge. To love means to revive the humanity of the others, to see them in their completeness and freedom, and then go into the details of our differences.

The need to dominate the other falls when affection comes first. Affection does not judge, but it encourages us to find one another and build together. When we love the other, we become better people. When we give, we receive. Love is the only equation in which if we have "2" and give "1," we get "4." It is always a win-win situation when we know that we are loved and respected, and have the opportunity to reciprocate.

The writer Luis Carlos Restrepo[4] says that we live in a time of emotional illiteracy; we have developed the highest technologies of the artificial intelligence at the expense of our attention to affection: "What characterizes and distinguishes us from the artificial intelligence is the ability for emotions, our emotional intelligence, for rebuilding the world, as well as the knowledge gained through the affective bonds that have an effect on us."

Neither machines nor science can replace what we can understand through the emotional component that characterizes any interpersonal relationship. To let

4.   *El derecho a la ternura*, Barcelona, Ediciones Península, 1997, p. 26.

ourselves be affected by the others is an inexhaustible source of knowledge.

And then he continues: "... there is so much emotional awkwardness accumulated in our culture, that it seems understandable that doctors would not treat their relatives or loved ones when they are sick, because they would lose accuracy in their technical judgments. The dissociation between cognition and affection has denied us the path of integration of these two areas, a path that would allow us to know more finely and in depth the more we involved our affections. I refer to the integration of knowledge that all ancient cultures described with the beautiful name of wisdom."[5]

This book, it is hoped, may help us acknowledge the emotional blunders that we may have inherited, and discover the immense happiness found in being welcomed by the other fully, ungrudgingly. In this way we will rebuild the world, at least our small worlds, which make up our universe.

In two voices: Francisco

Reasons for bonds

Those who know that they need the others are interested in building relationships with them. It's not an exclusively material or emotional need, in which I seek refuge or lean on another, like a cane to help me walk. We're talking about the human need in general, and of each of us in particular, to recognize that we are limited and incomplete from every perspective, not only mental and physical, but also spiritual and religious. No one of sound mind can identify himself as complete, self-sufficient, whole and limitless. In the face of the limit, the first step is—in the religious experience addressed in these pages—toward God, the only one complete (absolute) and that completes us. And the passage from the need

---

5. Ibidem.

for the transcendent to the need for the others, fellow travelers, men and women like ourselves, is very short.

Let me explain. From the perspective of the teachings of the Second Testament, the experience with God is closely linked to the love of neighbor. The first letter of John says the following:

> Whoever says, "I am in the light," while hating a brother or sister, is still in the darkness. Whoever loves a brother or sister lives in the light, and in such a person there is no cause for stumbling."[6]

Just as I need God, because of my being a creature and my experience of human frailty, the love of others is a sign of my encounter with God. It's not a mere psychological fact, but deeply ontological. The need for the other, whether affectively and culturally, close or distant, is a real need that challenges us and drives us to action; that is, to love.

The interpersonal bond of closeness and solidarity, the love for our neighbor (in more biblical terms) is the basis of all dialogue. Beyond the form it may take (a friendship born spontaneously or with the creative willingness or effort to get close to the other), it becomes a profoundly human and religious reality, inasmuch as it binds people among themselves, with the other, and with the Totally Other.

The more distant the other is from me, the more imperative the creative pursuit of a personal closeness becomes. Can we dispense with the "distant other" on our journey to achieve the fulfillment of the human experience? As Igino Giordani, thinker and political figure of the twentieth century, liked to say: I, the other and God are a triangle which cannot be separated.[7] My religious experience is not authentic if I don't prioritize love for

---

6. 1 John 2:9–10
7. Igino Giordani (1894–1980), a significant figure in the ecclesial, cultural and political life of Italy in the twentieth century. Writer and journalist, teacher and legislator.

the other, the icon of the Totally Other, source and fullness of our lives.

God as model of love

God for Christians is One and Triune at the same time. He is One but not alone, as his intimate life is relationship among distinct persons. It is the model of love as we Christians conceive it: a mutual love reached through the reciprocal self-giving of human beings, a love of such intensity that inclines to unite those who are different.

The Triune God is a mystery of the Christian faith that is difficult to understand. But we Christians find in the Trinity the religious motivations that encourage us to reach out to the others and that we must, gradually, translate into practice in order to improve the way we act. Why? Because for the Christian it should be evident that God calls us to communion with other people, with those who are different, for without this there is no real life or true human experience. We need each other in order to realize ourselves. The other is indispensable in our way to God.

Any reader might object that the experience of communion that Christianity proposes should project Christians toward all human beings and not specifically toward the Jews or a Jewish person in particular. In other words, why should Christians talk about the need to build bonds with Jews? While these considerations are legitimate, it is true, at the same time, that Vatican II highlights the specific ties that Christians have with Jews:

> The Church "cannot forget that she draws sustenance from the root of that well-cultivated olive tree onto which have been grafted the wild shoots, the Gentiles." And "... she acknowledges that, according to God's saving design, the beginnings of her faith and her election are found already among the Patriarchs, Moses and the prophets..."[8]

---

8.   NA 4.

Relationships, spaces for the presence of God

Interpersonal relationships, if based on the values that we have analyzed, are the adequate space for the growth of everyone. It is a growth that involves a better self-understanding of one's own religious experience, a greater openness to the experience of the other and, quite possibly, a sincere understanding for the way others conceive their rapport with God and with the world. It is a growth that involves us in a human and spiritual maturity, and makes us abandon a certain narrow-mindedness that prevents us from opening ourselves up fully to reality.

All this creative and prolific power that we have clearly seen in the experience of writing these pages opens up a space that allows a greater presence of God in our personal and interpersonal lives. It invites God's action.

In the words of Scripture, "Unless the Lord builds the house, those who build it labor in vain."[9] God is present in the construction of the house of dialogue. He is its main architect.

How could Jews and Christians otherwise get closer together after having been separated by significant theological issues and by centuries of misunderstandings, persecutions, and conflicts, with only the strength of the intelligence and the will of some individuals?

A selfless, friendly and creative relationship, which is faithful to listening to each other, allows God to inspire and implement actions of genuine dialogue and propose creative ideas. That is our experience.

The interpersonal bond cannot be closed in: it is always open to others, it is commitment to the others

The bond of dialogue, of "dialogical love," in the words of Paulo Freire, cannot be closed but it must lead to fecundity and dissemination. There is no true love

9.   Cf Psalm 127.1

without openness to new life and new spaces that create greater dialogue and understanding.

The bond between Jews and Christians, even among a single Jew and a single Christian, to the extent that it deepens and matures, is never sterile. Its effects can be verified in two key areas.

The first effect occurs within religious communities: dialogue is contagious and causes the participation of others. Many are attracted by the sincerity of the relationship and want to join in.

The second effect can be seen in the environment: dialogue opens the door to concrete actions in favor of society and a more united and fraternal humanity. It is what Silvina and I have experienced around us and in various places.

All of this is due to an interpersonal encounter in which the values of respect, trust and listening are applied, mutual esteem grows and, as a result, preconceptions fall. Every great light starts from a tiny spark, which spreads by its own nature.

Chapter 7

Removing Barriers and Prejudices in Dialogue

In unison: Francisco *and* Silvina

WE HAVE BEEN DISHEARTENED on our journey several times with respect to dialogue. Arguments circulate that rejected and discouraged it, connected perhaps to experiences of pain and failure when attempting it or to the fear of losing one's own identity. It seemed important to write down these experiences, to reflect on them and retrace their tracks, in an effort to understand why something that should be liberating and exhilarating becomes an uphill climb.

Each individual experience shapes our notion of dialogue and encounter. We are aware that we can't be naive and we have to face the hard edges of our proposal in order to move towards a genuine and deep dialogue.

The following pages contain experiences and phrases which might trouble some readers, although nothing is further from our intentions. At the same time, life has led us to understand that not everyone thinks as we do and not everyone uses words in the same way we use them. Furthermore, many do not dare get closer to the others because they harbor deeply rooted fears, insecurities and personal stories, which have led them away from this experience of dialogue. We will try to respond to each one of these obstacles, above all, with the witness of our own lives. In short, "layers of humanity" beneath the external forms may hinder going forward at times. We are aware that for one to be able to walk and advance, our journey needs small imbalances in order not to remain stagnant. Every step we take may threaten our stability, but should we then choose immobility?

Let's climb together over the obstacles that we think are slowing the progress of Jewish-Christian dialogue and confront them seriously. So many years of separation need to be addressed with patience and conviction.

In two voices: Silvina

Obstacle 1: "Dialogue wants me to convert to the religion of the other"

In 2002, my son Ariel was invited by the Focolare Movement to the Supercongress, a large meeting of teenagers from around the world for peace. Besides the great joy and surprise at the possibility of sharing with my son such an experience, I received some warnings. Yes, it was important that a 13-year shared a unique and once-in-a-lifetime experience somewhere in the world together with thousands and thousands of young people from other religions, nationalities, ethnicities, and political beliefs, learning how to see a brother or a sister in his neighbor and showing this experience of fraternity to the world. However, such an opportunity did not prevent disparaging comments, which we could consider as destructive of trust.

The phrase from relatives of mine which struck me the most was: "Be careful that they don't convert him." At first I had to think whether I was understanding what they were saying. Far from judging them, for they meant well, I realized that they revealed one of the obstacles for dialogue: the assumption that under the pretext of dialogue there is the ulterior motive to convert others. In this case, the view of these Jewish persons was that Catholics are always trying to "draw more water to their own mill" (turn things to their advantage), a suspicion that is theologically based since Christianity is missionary and has a vocation to universality, while Judaism is not.

Then I tried to decipher the imagery behind the warning: my son is going to be overwhelmed. He'll be with a Catholic majority that will "seduce" him. This kind of openness is not needed but in fact risky.

Believe me when I say that I understand this position, which has to do with our survival instinct and our search for security. However, I wonder whether the preservation of our religious identity is achieved by locking ourselves in and avoiding contact with others, or by strengthening our convictions in order to share them in the wider world. I wonder if the contact with others weakens me or gives me instead the tools to solidify my own identity and my own answers.

To finish this story and its message, I will tell you that Ariel, my son, got off the bus with the entire group of Christian boys from Argentina and they stayed at a hotel that also hosted the youth delegation from Burundi. I stayed on the bus since my hotel was in another part of town. I admit that I felt some trepidation. How would Ariel, the only Jewish boy, react amid so much diversity? Would he need me to avoid feeling alone? Would he feel alone? Would they know how to attend to him? Would they listen to him?

The next morning these questions were answered with the following account:

> When they went to sleep, the coordinator of the Argentine boys invited everyone to pray the Lord's Prayer. Then, Ariel asked, "What about me? I am also here with you and I do not pray the Our Father when I go to sleep!" How interesting, simple and deep! They were learning to live together, each having their own space. Immediately, the coordinator asked him what Jews prayed before bedtime and Ariel replied that their night prayer is called the *Shema Yisrael*: Hear, O Israel (Deuteronomy 6:4). So, Ariel said his prayer, accompanied by the silence of all and then he respectfully shared their Our Father.

As it is obvious, no one wanted to convert anyone. Everyone wanted to learn from the others, making room for them lovingly, getting to know their customs, and they were encouraged to share them in the same space.

It is a lesson that will accompany us throughout our lives.

In two voices: Silvina

Obstacle 2: "Our differences are so irreconcilable that it's not worth the effort to work on them"

More than once I meet good people, friends and relatives who, hearing of my activities and involvement in Jewish-Christian dialogue, express their distrust and lack of understanding of this endeavor.

Those who say they do not believe in this kind of dialogue justified their view by saying that there is an abyss between Jews and Christians, and that their historical and ideological differences (which, in Christian terms, we could call doctrinal or theological) cannot be analyzed with the same religious categories.

While for Christians the Messiah already came and further, he is God, son of God, because God is One and Three. For Jews, however, the Messiah has not yet come, and the very idea of the Trinity or the notion of a God incarnated in a human being is an image very difficult to assimilate.

This difference between the two religious traditions is not simply a minor matter. For Jews, Christians are not just "any" others. They are "others," who were once part of "our own selves" and left this home. On the other hand, seen from the simple perspective of many Christians, we could say that they regard Jews as those who refuse to see the truth and believe in the coming of the Redeemer, and who insist on an "old" (as the "Old Testament"), anachronistic view, which denies the new revelation.

To the Jew, the Christian is not just someone with a polytheistic worldview, philosophy or creed. No, he or she is a member of a religion that worships a Jew, but rejects circumcision and many other precepts of Jewish law. Christians claim to be the heirs of a new covenant and they study the Hebrew scriptures from a different perspective than the rabbinic tradition.[1]

It is clear that both Jews and Christians are known to be heirs of the biblical tradition. But the exegesis of the same texts is done in ways that at times mark the lines of division in both religious traditions. Let's take an example to understand what I mean:

> The example of Isaiah 7:14. Jewish tradition reads the verse in this way: "Therefore the Lord himself shall give you a sign: Behold, *a young woman* shall conceive and bear a son, and shall name him Emmanuel."

> Instead, in certain Christian translations it reads: "Therefore the Lord himself shall give you a sign: Behold, *a virgin* will conceive and bear a son, and shall name him Emmanuel."

In short, some may think that the prophecy of Isaiah regards a young woman who will give birth, while others will identify the young woman as the Virgin Mary, announcing the arrival of the Redeemer; all in the very same First Testament.[2]

1. We call rabbinic tradition to the exegesis after the canonization of Tanakh—the Hebrew Bible. It comprises the indications and explanations of the oral tradition interpreting the ambiguities and difficulties of the Biblical text. The oral law was codified and recorded for the first time in the third century, to prevent its loss in the diaspora; Judah the Prince wrote the first known comment on the interpretation of the law, the Mishnah, from the teachings of the *Tannaim*, sages of the oral tradition. At the same time, the content of the Mishnah was object of debate, discussion and commentary by the scholars of the Jewish communities in Israel and Babylon; the outcome of these discussions resulted in other volumes of commentaries, called Gemara. Along with the Mishnah, these volumes constitute the Talmud, the collection of rabbinic tradition.
2. By way of illustration we could clarify this by saying that the problem arises in the translation of the Hebrew word *"almah."* Biblical scholars agree that this word can mean 'virgin,' 'young woman of marriageable age,' 'maiden,' or 'just married.' Therefore, the word

The closeness between Jews and Christians and their sharing the same "first revealed text" makes things more difficult. It is easier to dialogue with those whom I have less in common than with those whom I share some areas, precisely because we look at them from such a different perspective. It is a difference that, in spite of sounding paradoxical, both unites and separates us.

For example, many Jews refuse to be addressed as the "elder brothers" or the "older brethren" of Christians, since it's a term that sounds pejorative. Some Jews say of Christians: "They left the family, later on they expelled us from their settings, and now it turns out that we are 'their brothers'?"

Such obstacles are anchored in our historical memory and in the personal experiences of many of us who live in countries with a Catholic majority, where some sectors of society have not or still do not welcome and accept the Jewish minority.

The distrust of many Jews regarding dialogue with Christians has a component of pain, a bitter taste for the imbalance in history and the uneven game played by the institutions which regulate the power of religion with regards to the majority and the minority (in their relationships with the State, for example). And it may also occur because they are afraid of a false interpretation of the original Jewish texts that Christians sometimes make, in the opinion of many Jews.

A Jewish intellectual and human rights activist once told me: "I do not feel that Christians are my brothers. I feel more comfortable with Muslims; they are like me."

What's the meaning of this comment? What is behind this decades-old attempt to find a common conversation

---

"almah" does not always mean 'virgin.' This word appears in some other parts of the First Testament and in all of them signifies 'maiden': Genesis 24:43, Exodus 2:8, Psalms 68:25, Proverbs 30:19, Song of Songs 1, 3 , 6 , 8. There is additionally another Hebrew word for "virgin" which is *"bethulah."* The Septuagint, the translation of the Hebrew Bible into Greek, prior to Christianity, translates the word *"almah"* as *"parthenos,"* word which in the Greek Spanish Lexicon is translated as "virgin."

and behind a certain sense of failure that overwhelms us (both Jews and Christians!), because of the manipulation, in some cases, or the apparent hypocrisy, in others?

More than one person has told me that those who engage in dialogue do not really believe in it in their hearts. They do it as a strategy of political correctness, but in the end, our living together does not improve because there are irremediable rifts between both traditions.

Writing these pages I review the answers in my mind: my attempts to explain why I feel it is not impossible, as well as the arguments to make clear that despite the gap, there is much firm ground on which to build bridges.

I conducted an exercise testing my own experience. I wondered: can I approach the Christian reality of Jesus from the paradigms and beliefs in which I was raised? Of course I understand it from the other's perspective and respect it as a category of the other's faith. But this does not make it less of a difference between us.

And yet, these very different worlds do not make me give up hope when it comes to dialogue. Perhaps we should accept that although it is difficult to grasp perfectly the essential truths of the religious tradition of the other, there is a compatible universe in which my spiritual life is enriched. And this happens when I find not only the gaps but also the simple and yet, immense fundamentals, appreciating the other's existence, in all of his or her expressions, overcoming any barriers and plunging into the divine manifestation represented by the other with peace of mind.

Being human, by definition, makes us diverse in many aspects of our lives. However, with regards to religious beliefs, our threshold for tolerance and the acceptance of our differences narrows considerably, as if we were to put in danger constitutive dimensions of our deepest being. Our ability to listen and understand diminishes when speaking about faith.

Perhaps the best, first step is not to search for our common origins or the justification for our "fraternity" because they are not able to conceal the fact that the separation was and continues to be traumatic.

Here, the first encounter belongs to one and to the other, different, unique, with a past history that must be heard and a present that calls to be built. There is no dialogue "by decree," but as we have been saying over and over again in these pages, we need people with the vocation to meet one another, with the desire to dive into the others' world and to know them without judging them—if they don't try to prove that what I think and believe is invalid. Perhaps the purpose of dialogue is neither to deal with nor to deny the differences.

This book will not soften the ideological or theological breach that separates our traditions, because the distance is a reality and because we do not pretend to do so. But it will allow us to look at each other from our own shore with more lucidity. If we find an abyss, dialogue will make sure that we will not fall into the void. At the same time, and because of all the advances that humanity has made, we have enough tools to raise bridges, build roads and open up many shared spaces that will positively challenge our relationship and our own learning.

In two voices: Francisco

Obstacle 3: "The dialogue does not let me express myself"

I heard many times from Christians committed to their faith and their church comments that can be summarized as follows:

> "We can dialogue with Jews only if we avoid talking about certain topics of our faith. If we start talking about Jesus and who he is for us, it causes discomfort and cuts off the other. Jews can fully express their tradition, and instead we feel obliged to refer only to the books of the Hebrew Bible. Frankly, we can't refer

> to Christian scriptures or the core of our faith, for example, the mystery of the Triune God or that God became incarnate in Jesus."

One could say that, in the dialogue between Jews and Christians, this type of comment touches a raw nerve. This is a real obstacle in dialogue, it's not just a bogus remark. We could fill an entire library on the subject and go on endlessly analyzing it in depth.

I give only a few elements that have helped me overcome this obstacle.

First, Christians need to face a reality: dialogue is not symmetrical. It involves the recognition of asymmetries of all kinds: exegetical, theological, historical, sociological and psychological. Jewish tradition and Christianity are not like those wooden double doors in some old houses that are mostly symmetrical with just a few slight differences (a lock in one side, a curtain in the other). It would be more appropriate to compare them with an apple tree and an elm. Both are trees and bear fruit, but they are not cared for in the same way, their flowers are different, they don't yield fruit at the same time, they grow in different terrain, etc. Both are trees, obviously, but they should be considered both in their differences and in their similarities.

From a purely religious perspective, we Christians tend to think that Jews possess our same religious categories, our same language and way of living and expressing the faith, with the only exception that we have different reasons for our beliefs. However, study and experience indicate that Jews and Christians have very different ways of relating to faith in general and to sacred texts in particular. This does not mean that we can't "understand" or at least come near to the way Judaism relates to God, the sacred texts and its tradition. But for this we must open our minds and hearts to religious and cultural categories different from our own: radically different. Being aware of these diversities and asymmetries makes closeness easier.

Another element to consider is of an historic nature. In the first years of Jewish-Christian dialogue (mid-twentieth century), a phrase was coined that is still valid: "The faith of Jesus unites us but the faith in Jesus separates us." Jesus' historical, cultural and religious context can be both an element for understanding and a point of separation because both traditions deployed different interpretations of the same texts and even of the same facts.

Christians must recognize that the *kerygma*[3] of Christianity, the faith in Jesus' death and resurrection, is a very complex concept to understand within the cultural and religious categories of Jews.

Christianity and rabbinic tradition, more or less contemporaneously, have approached the Hebrew Bible in different ways. Some scholars have ventured to say that the rabbinic tradition clearly distanced itself from all those interpretations of the First Testament that were close to Christian positions.[4] Moreover, the long process of inculturation of the Christian faith in the Greek milieu opened an even wider cultural gap, so that Christians and Jews began to speak, symbolically and literally, two different languages.

Leaving aside the academic debate, which would involve several libraries and never-ending discussions, there is an inescapable distance between Christians and Jews as to the interpretation of the same biblical texts.

Moreover, history confirms that in the name of Jesus of Nazareth, Christian groups committed many injustices and atrocities, especially against Jews: ghettoization, persecutions, and massacres. Christian thinkers of the first centuries helped sow and nurture seeds of anti-Semitism that are still present in many sectors of Western society.[5]

---

3. *kerygma*, a Greek word meaning the announcement of the "Good News" of Christianity.
4. Vidal Manzanares, C., *El judeo-cristianismo palestino en el siglo I. De Pentecostés a Jamnia*, Madrid, Trotta, 1995.
5. D'Auria, María Teresa, *Re-spectus, Judaísmo y conciencia cristiana*,

It is logical, then, for some, that the reference to Jesus and his teaching is reminiscent of persecutions and stigmatizations, attempts of forced conversion,[6] prejudice and enormous suffering. That's why it's not easy for them to hear about Jesus or the Christian faith. Indeed, when Christians wield theoretically the precepts of charity and brotherhood, as we do sometimes rather superficially, this can be interpreted as hypocritical, if read in the arch of the centuries of Judeo-Christian relations or "anti-relations."

I hope these lines have not tired the reader. I believe they were necessary in order to explain the reason why when we speak about Christianity to Jews, without having heard them fully first and understood something of their life, we may find a certain rejection on their part.

The situation is quite different when Christians — in an attitude of trust, listening and affection that has previously been created, with the result of being able to capture some of the sensitivity of the other — speak of their own religious experience with humility and respect, seeking words that do not hurt. They will certainly be able to express themselves fully without causing rejection.

A personal anecdote:

> A friend of mine, a rabbi, invited me for Sabbath dinner at his home. I was not the only guest. There were also present a couple of Jewish psychoanalysts, very open and friendly but with very little knowledge about Christianity. At one point during dinner they began to ask me leading questions about Christianity and the Church: Why can't priests marry? How do they live their sexuality? Why do Christians talk so much about love while the Church does not allow priests to marry? Why do Christians say that Jesus resurrected? Their questions were different in nature,

---

Montevideo, Ed. Confraternidad Judeo-Cristiana del Uruguay, 2004, pp. 91 to 105.

6. As an example, it is enough to remember the Jewish Shylock in "The Merchant of Venice" by William Shakespeare.

some theological, some regarding church organization, but when asked at the same time, they proved to be overwhelming. I was uncomfortable. I also remember the discomfort of my rabbi friend and his wife because of the unusual "tribunal" to which I was being subjected.

The end of this story is much less important than sharing the reflection it may provoke. In front of situations like these, we can always respond in different ways. If we shut down in our discomfort, judging our questioners negatively, without trying to step beyond our first impression, we will surely conclude that dialogue is almost impossible. But if we are prepared and we venture to try to understand the motivations that lead to questions of this nature, we will find the answers with greater clarity and precision, without renouncing our views and beliefs. And this will promote dialogue.

In two voices: Silvina

Obstacle 4: "Jews don't need to dialogue with Christians to live as Jews, but Christians do"

Some years ago I was part of the faculty of a course called "History of Religions." There, representatives of every religious tradition taught the basics of each faith to a large group of students. Upon completion of the school year, all of us teachers took part in a kind of roundtable approach to address the issue of dialogue among our various religions. For several years I was part of this beautiful experience. From among many stories I could share with you and the many lessons that I learned from my students, I would like to tell one that may help shed light on the obstacle we will try to address in the next pages.

A student and now dear friend would come to ask me lots of questions at the end of each class and would take notes on every answer I gave her. The first year of classes ended. When I returned to teach the course to another group during the following year, I met her, Silvia Mongiardino, again. I asked her what was she doing there and she said she still had many questions, and that she realized that the more she knew about Judaism, the more she understood and loved her religion, Christianity.

The story has a wonderful ending. At the end of the second year, she told me she was a painter and that the inspiration of my classes had led her to paint each of the topics I taught, turning every lesson into a work of art. I told her, tearfully, that it was the best homage I could have ever received as a teacher and as a Jew, and that it would be very important to get it published. Finally it came to light in the form of a book called *A Shared God,* which we presented in a parish and in a synagogue. At the end of the first book presentation, a friend of the artist flipped through the book until the last pages seeking the shift from Judaism to Christianity, but it just so happened that the book dealt only with Jewish themes. Then I heard that the friend asked the artist: "And where is Jesus in this book?" and she answered wisely: "You are reading him."

The life of dialogue gives these little flashes of divine light and fills us with experiences that mark us forever, like the one I had just shared with you.

Why do I tell such a beautiful story when we are speaking of obstacles? I will explain:

> When Silvia told me that she loved Christianity more after having learned in depth the fundamentals of Judaism, I had two thoughts. The first was logical: many Gospel stories, the ritual practices of Jesus and the Apostles, and even several sermons, are better understood when the original source which inspired Jesus to develop his vision and vocation is known. The second lesson was more existential. I felt this was a likely path to start a "two-way street" in our dialogue: my Judaism was good for her and I loved that what I had to offer was welcomed in such a way. We were both inspired because we found a shared space.

From the Christian point of view, my Judaism was not being rejected but was a starting point for understanding the developing of the Christian tradition.

With this story and reflection I try to respond to those who say that Christians need to dialogue with Jews in order to be Christians because Jesus and his surroundings were Jewish; on the other hand, Jews have no need to dialogue with or deepen their knowledge of Christianity since no aspect of this religion nourishes the tradition of Israel.

It is like this, undoubtedly, in historical terms. The matter then remains whether we try to get close to the other only when there is a practical gain. From a purely informational perspective, it's true I'm not going to learn more about Judaism if I know more about Christianity. But I could say with certainty that, when I dialogue with the Christian world, when I am able to answer their questions, when I am able to create a meeting space that values humanity over any dispute or difference, I learn much from myself and my Jewish beliefs. Both traditions have as a religious mandate to love the other, and the possibility of putting it into practice only comes about when I build spaces with the other, beyond the apparent "gains." I feel the doors are opened for a space of dialogue each time I had the opportunity to study the Gospel and discover how some of Jesus' sermons are in agreement with rabbinic teachers from his time such as the sage Hillel. Or when I understand the exegesis that Jesus did on some topics of the Torah, by choosing the "Twelve" and with them the symbol of the "Twelve Tribes of Israel."

As I like to say in these pages, dialogue does not have for me a utilitarian purpose but it aims at a transcendent goal. I don't do it because of a particular benefit, but because the mere fact of devoting time to it dignifies my existence. Everything can be learning and gain if I don't close myself in and if I look for and find ways to get close to the other.

In two voices: Francisco

Obstacle 5: "There is never progress in dialogue"

As Rabbi Leon Klenicki (1930–2009) liked to say, it is necessary to go beyond the stage of "tea and charm" in Judeo-Christian relations and seek deeper understandings. In fact, he had been studying the Christian texts of the Apostle Paul in order to deepen the theological foundations of Judeo-Christian understanding.

Clearly the conciliar declaration *Nostra Aetate* signified a major breakthrough in our relations. Moreover, it represented a 'before and after' in the rough road travelled by Jews and Christians over the centuries. In fact, the entire Second Vatican Council entailed a substantial step forward, a real revolution in the relations between the two religions. We can bring to mind, by way of example, the Dogmatic Constitution *Lumen Gentium*, Number 16, which recognizes the special bond of Israel with Christians, or the decree *Dignitatis Humanae* on religious freedom.

Subsequent documents of the Catholic Church such as the "Notes on the correct way to present the Jews and Judaism in preaching and catechesis in the Roman Catholic Church" or the "Guidelines..." (cited several times in these pages) were also important milestones that allowed for a better unraveling of the exact scope of *Nostra Aetate*. The same is true of the important document *"We Remember: a Reflection on the Shoa,"* published in 1989 by the Vatican Commission for Religious Relations with the Jews.

Someone described the visit of John Paul II to the Synagogue of Rome as the longest trip of his pontificate (despite having travelled only a few hundred meters from the Vatican). That simple gesture brought down centuries of barriers and was very well regarded throughout the Jewish world.

Other important moments were the recognition of the state of Israel by the Vatican in 1993 (the Fundamental

Agreement marking that recognition was signed in 1993. The formal exchange of ambassadors took place in 1994), the trip of John Paul II to the land of Israel and the major apology to the Jewish people, both in the year 2000.

In the 50 years since the Vatican Council, we have seen a consolidation of the overtures of both sides towards the other, especially by the religious authorities. Therefore, it's incorrect to say that the dialogue between Jews and Christians "has not advanced" or "doesn't progress."

It is probably a legitimate aspiration to wish that dialogue may advance faster, take root deeper in our respective religions and be joined by more and more people and religious sectors. However, after centuries of misunderstanding and persecution, it must be acknowledged that the steps taken by both Christians and Jews toward each other are huge.

Actually, I think that the alleged sense of stagnation has to do with a subjective perception as well as deeply-rooted mental structures and ideas regarding the other, which are difficult to remove from the mind and soul of many. We have been saying it in these pages again and again; documents and official acts do not guarantee a change of consciousness.

Take for example the great act of reconciliation made by John Paul II, which was at the basis of his request for forgiveness. At that time, the Holy Father said:

> "The act carried out today is a sincere acknowledgment of the faults committed by the children of the Church in the remote and recent past, and a humble supplication for God's forgiveness. This will no doubt awaken consciences, enabling Christians to enter the third millennium more open to God and his plan of love."

We could engage in a great philosophical discussion regarding the value of apologizing for things that others did. Or instead, we could simply recognize that our

actions, especially if they are made in the name of religion, are not merely individual, but have such an impact on the group to the point of leaving a mark, which
later—collectively—we have to overcome. In this context, it is perfectly understandable that this "first step"
that John Paul II took was on behalf of Catholics toward
Jews, who had been victims, often times, of actions by
Christians.

The big question is whether these words so important for the history of humanity, expressed by the top of
the pontifical hierarchy, were enough to produce a true
revolution concerning forgiveness and its practical ap-
plications.

In my view, this is the crux of the matter: many
words are said but very few are translated into action.
Many Christians lamented this apology, because it regarded faults they hadn't committed. For many Jews, it
was difficult to believe that the sincere request for forgiveness of John Paul II would have any impact on the
entire Christian community.

What does it take to embody words of reconciliation
and acceptance of the other in our daily lives? As we
have said in these pages, it takes time, a decision not
to be stuck with old, collective stigmas and having the
courage to get to know the other.

Jews and Christians have inherited an old family
fight which drags on and extends beyond their real ties.
We must face reality with all its nuances: the legacy we
carry, the fears transmitted to us, with the hope of knowing that the possibility to return to embrace one another
and sit down to listen to the truths of the other exists
within ourselves.

We still have a long way to go, of course, but we are
on the road.

In unison: Francisco *and* Silvina

Obstacle 6: "Why keep innovating and proposing new forms of dialogue?"

In a current social context of relativism concerning truths that once seemed to be deep-rooted and strong, it seems almost natural to expect the risk of a pendulum effect that would deny any openness to what is new and would lead to a radical assertion of our personal or institutional identity, whether national or religious. This phenomenon has led religious people, both Christian and Jewish, to wonder whether to continue on the path of dialogue, creating opportunities, opening spaces and innovating or, instead, return to a consolidation of our own particular religious identity and, thus, avoid the risk of openness, which, it is said, can confuse and disrupt. It is a common line of thinking nowadays and a real obstacle to dialogue.

Dialogue requires both openness to the reality of the other and a solid religious identity. In order to meet the other, I must know where they are. To dialogue with others, I must identify and recognize their space of faith and their personal and community religious experience.

These two elements, openness and solidity of one's own identity, must have a healthy tension between them. If one is missing, dialogue gets distorted, risking to turn to syncretism or to a false irenicism,[7] peace at any cost, superficial and rootless, or, conversely, dialogue can be rejected due to fundamentalism or a denial of the identity of the other.

Furthermore, dialogue requires openness to the reality of the other, as mentioned earlier, and also requires openness to our own reality. Sometimes we get stuck in old structures that had already ceased to be useful in our own traditions. We remain rooted in exegeses that were produced at other times, pursuing certain goals or facing

---

7. An irenecist attitude is that of one who tries to create or preserve peace by simply avoiding confrontation. It is like an irresponsible and rather comfortable tolerance.

problems that are not relevant today. We continue to live in a "present past," an "uncritical now," without giving a thought to the more appropriate questions of "who we are and who we want to be."

Regarding the question about why innovating is important, the answer is: because we are alive! And the consciousness of life calls for our existence to be happy, whole, forward-looking and to take a step there where our ancestors could not, in those landmarks of history in which pain, damage or silence was caused because of many circumstances.

The famous saying of Heraclitus of Ephesus: "No one steps in the same river twice, for it's not the same river and it's not the same man," helps explain that we are beings in motion, we grow and mature in a historic time, which is being created by either our actions or our lethargy. The river, that is, the present time, flows and we also change in the process.

What does it depend on? It depends on multiple factors, both collective and personal. The feeling that we have is that the present time is encouraging for dialogue between Jews and Christians and that our relationships are more mature. The existential rivalries, which will live in the memory, cannot be construed as the only possible distinguishing mark among both religious traditions.

We need to "innovate," to find ways and opportunities for encounter, to grow in the understanding of the other, to strengthen our own religious identity because we believe that the encounter with the other fortifies our own convictions.

The result of this decision will be the peace of mind and the satisfaction of having dared to look at each other differently.

It's something really possible and we can give witness to it. No one is safer at home than he who has the peace of mind to leave the door open because he trusts his neighbors.

Lessons along the way

During the writing of the book, when dealing with subjects that we agreed with, our writing flowed effortlessly. We would meet in order to discuss and develop these ideas that eventually were transformed into the text. However, this chapter was different. Another dynamic was necessary when we confronted difficulties, entrenched positions, and obstacles to dialogue that were different for both Jews and Christians. We learned that it was important to say everything we wanted to say, in the best way, obviously, but without avoiding the harshness of the situations. Later, each one's text was read by the other, from one's own viewpoint. This guaranteed a sensitive reading from the other's position. There were many corrections, debates and the fear of sometimes offending by exposing difficulties deeply entrenched in our co-religionists. The amendments to our texts had to do primarily with the sensitivity of language in order to avoid stigmatizing generalizations. We can also attest that the affection and trust helped us address the most complex issues and that the loving and respectful gaze of the other was always a source of inspiration and learning.

Chapter 8

Inward Dialogue
Intra-community Dialogue

In two voices: Francisco

Intra-community dialogue: a training school for interfaith dialogue

WHERE DO CHILDREN LEARN to live with others, deal with their differences and solve conflicts with those who are alike and different from them? First, they do this within the core of their own family. Later on, as they grow, they will do this learning in other social settings such as the school, the youth group, etc.

The family, especially fraternal relationships, is the context where children learn to process the conflicts of interest, to open their own spaces and respect the spaces of the others from a psychological and sociological point of view. The presence of others allows the child to understand that, sooner or later, he or she must coexist with them, and that living together is fruitful and wonderful and those others will accompany one throughout life.

This analogy of the human family is well applicable in the religious sphere. Indeed, the function of religion is to unite people more closely with God and with each other. Religious search is never individual: it is in the very essence of the religious reality to secure a bond between people, a strong bond that will allow them to recognize themselves as part of a "family" united by ties which form the relationship with God and with the world. Religions are necessarily community spaces composed of persons connected by their relationship with the divine, a true, all-inclusive family that strives to be united. And in order to achieve it, it needs a common search for truth and for processing differences; in short, it needs dialogue.

Dialogue within our own religion is a true training for interreligious dialogue. This was expressed by Rev. Daniel Martínez[1] in his presentation during the Judeo-Christian Symposium of August 2012:[2] "The intra-community dialogue serves as a training ground in order to learn interreligious dialogue as a 'lifestyle' and its tools."

We will unravel these statements. If young people grow up in religious circles where they can search for and work out their differences together, without allowing what separates them to be stronger than what unites them, and if this is lived honestly, they will be carrying out a natural school of dialogue. This will allow them to grow in their ability to encounter others who are not their "co-religionists." Dialogue will become a "life-style" that is projected outward from within the religious group. As Martínez expresses it: "... to dialogue among those we agree with is the easiest way to learn how to discuss in order to find points in common, clearly and respectfully express our view of things and listen to others unconditionally." These are obviously ideals to aim at and roads to travel on, and that is what this book is all about.

Obtaining the tools for dialogue

There is another reason by which the practice of fraternity in the space of one's own religion is an indispensable basis for finding ties with others of common humanity and different religions. It is in the area of our own religion where we learn the tools to reach out to those who are different. This is where we receive the

---

1. Daniel Martínez Suárez (1965), Licentiate of Biblical Theology. Professor of Sacred Scripture and Biblical Languages at the Faculty of Theology of Montevideo.
2. O'Higgins, Buenos Aires, August 21–25, 2012.

necessary training to enter into dialogue with the other, either from a spiritual point of view (think of the Christian commandments of love of neighbor) and also from a doctrinal and institutional point of view (it is sufficient to consider *Nostra Aetate* and other documents of the Catholic Church).

The process of configuration of our own religious identity, which necessarily passes through training and dialogue within the community, offers the conceptual and affective tools needed to take on ways to dialogue with those who are outside the visible boundaries of our religious community. It enables us to dialogue with them. Without a strong identity, forged in the crucible of the dialogic space of our own community, it becomes difficult to take the path of interreligious dialogue.

Expressions of intra-community dialogue

We Christians have a transcendent foundation that drives us to intra-community dialogue, whether it be spaces of dialogue within the Catholic Church or those that promote approaching other churches and Christian ecclesial communities (what we call "ecumenical dialogue"). It lies in the so-called "testament of Jesus" found in the Gospel of John (17:21): "Father, may they all be one." Jesus makes this request to his Christian disciples, who must be "one" in order to be able to reach out to others. This unity is not uniformity and is graphically expressed by the apostle Paul in his letter to the Galatians:

> For you were called to freedom, brothers and sisters; only do not use your freedom as an opportunity for self-indulgence, but through love become slaves to one another. For the whole law is summed up in a single commandment, 'You shall love your neighbor as yourself.' If, however, you bite and devour one another, take care that you are not consumed by one another.[3]

---

3. Galatians 5:13–15.

Interreligious dialogue, however, is carried out by individuals, and it is always institutional because religions themselves are institutional. Without this dimension of the institution, interfaith dialogue will be a witness to mutual charity (as Martínez stated in the presentation cited earlier) even an authentic prophetic cry, but it will not be interfaith dialogue. If those in charge of dialoguing do not represent in some way the members of their religion, full conditions for dialogue will not have been reached.

However, it is also true that dialogue develops at various levels and therefore I am not suggesting to rule out personal initiative, which bears so many fruits. Indeed, behind each person, a Christian or a Jew, there is a collective that identifies with that religion. It is a legacy that we all carry and we must be aware of it in order to properly respond to it.

A religious space

The intra-community dialogue is religious space and it opens a space for communion, as Christians would say, which must reach its fullness, because it allows the true community to search for the Face of God. In the mouth of the Psalmist: "'Come,' says my heart, 'seek his face;' your face, LORD, do I seek! Do not hide your face from me."[4] That Face we know is infinitely more than what we may think, say, or experience of Himself .

By virtue of this, then, the door is open to interfaith dialogue. In the words of Benedict XVI: "... the need for all those who believe in God to join in seeking peace, to attempt to draw closer to one another, and to journey together, even with their differing images of God, towards the source of Light—this is interreligious dialogue."[5]

---

4. Ps 27, 8:9.
5. Benedict XVI, "Letter to the Bishops," March 10, 2009.

In two voices: Silvina

Intra-community dialogue: a daily exercise of fraternity

Dad, what does it mean to be Jewish?
Those born in France are French without a doubt.
Those born in Italy
don't wonder why they are Italian.
And the Israelis are simply Israelis.
But the Jewish condition is not understood perfectly
or recorded in documents.
One is not born Jewish unexpectedly;
it's not an easy birth;
darkness on one side, a door that is crossed,
all of a sudden, light on the face.
We are born little by little,
discovering within slowly.
Centuries of struggle and pain and joy repressed;
millennia of grandeur and poetry
and people and love and faith in man
and integrity and falls and starting again
as a Jew;
not as a shadow born by chance
in any corner of the earth.
We are part of a restless people, in motion,
dispersed across the borders of five continents
for many centuries
as so many peoples evaporated
after having lost their collective memory.
But oddly, over mountains and oceans,
in two millennia of exile,
there were always Jews
who maintained their roots awakened
and did not deliver their entrails into oblivion...

Eliahu Toker, "Jewish Saga"[6]

These lines from a piece of Argentinean Jewish literature beautifully depict the question asked by many

---

6. Published by Arte y Papel, Buenos Aires, AR, 1973.

about what it means to be Jewish, who the Jews are, how they can be a people and live as citizens in many countries, whether or not they are a religion, how they function if there is not a central authority governing them.

These are questions that many rightly have regarding a condition that broke with the typical definition of people, nation, religion, community, and so on.

"We are part of a restless people in motion, dispersed across the borders of five continents," says the poet. We are one and many at the same time, because of two millennia of dispersion and countless factors that made us understand the sacred texts, the faith, the membership and practices in diverse and multiple ways, in an effort to respond to the prevailing leadership and discourse of the societies where we Jews have settled. The State of Israel was proclaimed in 1948, and a central, symbolic and real space was recovered, which must be added to the totality of plural voices that make up what many call "Judaism," and that I prefer to call "Jewish traditions or Judaisms." Each group, whether national, religious, or ideological,[7] has its rightful space and adherents within the Jewish people. This is due, I think, to the fact that the constant search of a definition and a consistency in the direction we want to take, each one carrying the legacy received by our ancestors, has kept us attentive, erudite, yearning to find a modern sense to the ancestral mandate. This multiplicity and versatility of what can't be exclusively defined as the Jewish condition brings about a great challenge: how to learn to converse among brothers who are located at different latitudes within the map of being Jewish.

The community foundation of dialogue

How to converse with other Jews who did not choose my option or who, at times, do not validate it? How to enter into dialogue with those I find it hard to have a

---

7. I prefer to leave the definitions without labels inasmuch as trying to classify the different movements and positions within Judaism would need to be elaborated in another way.

relationship with because of having interpreted the mandate of being Jewish in a totally different way from mine? In spite of all these apparent differences and distances, there is a concrete fact: we are all brothers and sisters and solely for this reason, we ought to try.

"What unites us is that we belong to the same people," it is often said. It would be very simple if this answer were enough. The problem lies in defining what a people is.

And I dare say that in the situation in which we Jews find ourselves for centuries, what keeps us together as a people is the challenge of entering into conversations, exchanging common ideas between siblings, between people who belong to the same family.

The content of this conversation is the enduring determination of the Jewish people to survive as a living narrative, as a collective and as a culture: the search for an answer is what binds us.

All Jews are responsible for one another.[8] The Talmud characterizes belonging to the Jewish collective in terms of "responsibility." We are to compensate for the others' mistakes and meet their needs and demands. We are compelled to help and stand up for one another regardless of our own ways of practicing Judaism. We are brothers and sisters and we are guarantors, and in this spirit, the dialogue between the different manifestations of Jewishness strengthens this mandate.

The obligation associated with being a community

We are a Jewish community when we feel responsible for each other, when we are willing to cooperate helpfully and to interrelate. And what better way to connect than the loving and respectful dialogue between the different groups that make up this community?

In this respect, an author who develops a very interesting concept is the Italian writer Roberto Esposito, who defines the word "community" from the concept of

8.   Shavuot 39a of the Babylonian Talmud.

143

munus, which is an obligation, a debt to the other. "From here it emerges, that *communitas* is the totality of persons united not by a 'property' but precisely by an obligation or a debt."[9] This debt binds us to the other, is an obligation I must fulfill, a bond not based on possessions but on compliance to the other. The starting point of this condition is precisely the acceptance of the non-ownership of oneself. And when one is installed in this position to accept that what is at stake in the interrelation is not the possession, that is, the possession of the absolute truth, then dialogue is really possible. From this perspective, intra-community dialogue is what allows us to interweave networks and establish ties between many subjects in order to transform us into stewards of one another.

Sometimes it is easier to engage in casual or friendly relations with those outside of our family, because what's at stake may not jeopardize our convictions. When we talk about members of the same household who have chosen different paths, sometimes the road gets steeper.

But the peace of finding high points of harmony and respect is invaluable. The Psalmist said it with the most appropriate words: "How good and how pleasant it is, when brothers dwell together as one!" (Psalm 133:1)

The dialogue between brothers is good, pleasant, constructive, edifying for our children and for those who don't belong to our people but recognize our capacity for fraternal conversations.

I won't say that "dialogue strengthens us" because this assertion generally implies the need for joining together in the face of an external danger. And I wouldn't want to propose an internal union in order to respond to a threat from outside. But what I can truly affirm is that intra-community dialogue strengthens us as human beings, dignifies our Jewish condition to us and to the world, reinforces our values, allows us to learn, nurture,

---

9. Esposito, Roberto, Communitas. *The Origin and Destiny of Community,* Stanford University Press, Stanford, California, 2010, p. 6.

develop, and to question and redefine ourselves, again and again.

Dialogue, Gratuitous Love

The Rabbinic tradition wonders why the Second Temple of Jerusalem was destroyed and it challenges the common notion that what provoked the annihilation and exile was the needless hatred between "brothers." To that common notion we must respond that if hate destroys, then gratuitous love builds, is fruitful and gives life. One of the consequences of a profound and sincere dialogue between brothers is that it causes a torrent of love that demands no reward. The dialogue between brothers does not pretend to divert the truth or erase the differences between them, but it is based on the ability to develop the good gaze and the good listening, and the virtue of respecting others even when we have chosen different roads within the same map. I do not intend by this to promote a state stripped of tensions. The constant search for definitions and arguments keeps us up to date and alive. What I really propose is that, along with that search for legitimacy of our own belonging, we develop the free and loving ability to allow our brothers to carry their own arguments and definitions, with the hope that we may come to share our visions of what Jewishness stands for and, thus, nurture each other.

Chapter 9

Real and Ideal Dreams

> And he dreamed that there was a ladder set up on the earth, the top of it reaching to heaven; and the angels of God were ascending and descending on it.
>
> *Genesis 28:12*

In unison: Francisco *and* Silvina

WHEN DID WE START to dream? Maybe since we were created; perhaps it is a characteristic of God's creation; He made us capable of dreaming. The biblical story tells us about the first person who describes a dream and realizes it is an image that does not belong to reality, but it teaches him much about this dimension. That was Jacob, who lies down to sleep in a place called Luz and dreams of a ladder grounded here on earth with its top in heaven and God's angels going up and down on it. And when Jacob awakes, he says: "God is in this place and I did not know it" and he called that place Bethel, "the house of God." Beyond the very rich exegesis we could do on this lovely passage from Genesis, we want to point out a detail in order to note that Jacob is not mentioned: "And he dreamed that there was a ladder set up on the earth, the top of it reaching to heaven...."

Who had the dream? From the wording of the text, it is Jacob. But from a more symbolic reading we could say that any of us can be the subject of this sentence. Furthermore, any of us has the right to dream, because every dream, every longing transformed into a vision is like a ladder, resting upon the ground near our feet, with its other end lost in the heights of heaven. When we dare to dream of things that help us bring a bit of heaven to earth, then the very same divinity is present.

We could define ourselves, with humility and happiness, as dreamers, as you will have noticed throughout this book, because we don't stop believing that a closer connection to heaven is possible, that dialogue has a great deal to teach us and that the closeness to and knowledge of others improves our lives.

That's why we decided to call this last chapter of our book "Real and ideal dreams," because even the highest of ideals starts becoming a reality when we have the courage to dream it.

And it's true, there are obstacles, many centuries of painful history, many rooted stigmas, prejudices and fears. But there are also belief, hope, commitment, willingness, affection. Gold and clay placed on the same tray for us to choose.

Perhaps our most real and ideal dream is to transform this subject of interreligious dialogue (to break down such a broad term, we could speak of interreligious knowledge, exploration, quest, encounter, research, discovery, construction), into transversal, cross-disciplinary subjects. Generally, we think of cross-disciplinary issues in school and formal education settings, where we aim at contents that are not limited to a school course or simply learning some technical skills. Education on cross curricular topics seeks a profound transformation of the person and is focused mostly on matters that respond to important social issues, such as the subject of gender, multiculturalism.

When we dream of a cross-disciplinary interreligious dialogue we imagine that religious affiliation can cross through the different areas of the life of any of us, without fixations, but also without having to hide it.

When we dream of a transversal approach, we dream of schools where students can share their religious experiences and communicate to each other, naturally and without risks, how they celebrate their religious holidays, their concepts of death, their main beliefs. When we confine religious matters only to religious institutions, children and young people who attend "secular" schools are not considered in one of their most profound characteristics, the religion they profess. There is no dialogue when there are no spaces to enable it. And as other diversities are taken into account, such as the countries of origin of the family, their typical food or the soccer clubs they root for, the religious affiliation is a distinctive feature of each boy and girl, which sometimes they must relinquish during school hours. Even families who do not profess a religion have given their children an argument, a content to justify their choice, which would be great to share with the rest of their peers with whom they live most of the day and most of their lives.

Over the last years, for example, the great struggle of indigenous peoples put on the agenda the concept of multiculturalism and of education in diversity. And the inclusion of these issues within the educational establishment changed the way we view the members of these indigenous peoples. Knowledge of their history and their worldview led to a greater support for their cause and to a much stronger social inclusion.

Therefore, we would like to propose to start in the school setting. When children don't attend class because they are celebrating a holy day on the religious calendar of their family, it would be wonderful to accompany them with empathy, respect and understanding as they commemorate a special day for their faith.

Religious diversity is as multifaceted as ethnic, cultural, and social diversity, among many others. It is constitutive of each person. The diversity of others enriches our lives. When in school settings we will be able to speak with ease and joy about our own and others' religion, we won't need books any longer that speak of dialogue, because it will have already happened spontaneously.

We believe that our society is mature enough to embark on the realization of this dream. Mutual exchange of religious experiences is not in contradiction with the true spirit of secularism. On the contrary, dialogue, when it is far-reaching and authentic, promotes the freedom of each and every one, encourages equality and dignity and paves the way for brotherhood.

We dream that working on these issues in training and educational settings may increase the sensitivity to the problems caused by prejudices and the view of suspicion and disrepute about those who don't profess our faith.

We dream of places of academic training that will contribute to the creation of contents and methodologies to address these topics, but mainly to prepare people for sensitive and respectful connections among each other.

We dream of formation that is intercultural and interreligious, starting with the academic centers that call themselves religious, and especially those places (seminaries, theological faculties and pastoral centers) that train ministers and religious leaders.

We dream that religious diversity may be studied and investigated in order to approach it and judge it by its content, rather than by inherited prejudices.

We dream of schools that feel free to call leaders of different religious faiths to meet students to discuss the basics of each faith and to demystify prejudiced and stigmatized images.

We dream of a country where religiosity is a fact of the present that can contribute to the great goals of this society when summoned to dialogue and to the spiritual dimension, and not confined to stagnant imaginary or anachronistic practices.

We dream that synagogues and parishes will develop joint activities to meet and go into depth, with teaching personnel that live out their ideal of a more deeply rooted religion precisely because it is in contact with the religious traditions of their neighbors.

We dream that public opinion may no longer select only news that ties religions to fundamentalism, and that all who belong to a loving spirituality may also be bearers of a message of brotherhood and hope.

We dream that communication professionals may be trained in religious subjects and know how to transmit them to the public in a more complete and refined fashion. That they may have awareness of everything that happens in the religious spectrum and not just those emerging pathologic aspects — to be undoubtedly considered, but which are many times overstated by the media's "magnifying lens" — which run the risk of erasing other news or positive achievements that continually take place in the field of religion and of interreligious dialogue.

We dream that we can confront the frenzy of this accelerated life with the necessary calm to enable us to think, feel and take the time to define the core values that sustain our life. In this reflection, our religious traditions have many resources to offer.

We dream that this time in history, which has dared to speak about diversity, can also include talk about pluralism: particular singularities which are summoned in a plural space in which each one has its place. The concept of religious pluralism advocates for the promotion and defense of religious freedom. And interreligious dialogue is an experience of freedom, the freedom to speak about myself and the other's freedom to be listened to. The freedom to practice my faith and for the others to do the same. The freedom to draw near the other in order to build a better world together, a world of shared human values beyond religious differences.

We dream that every religious tradition may find its own way to get close to the other. Time will be necessary in order to self-review and self-rediscover our convictions and messages to the world in which we live.

We dream that the issues arising as a result of inter-religious dialogue may be a source of responses to the important challenges that humanity faces today.

They are dreams, it's true, but they are not chimeras because there is nothing as constructive and transforming as that profound yearning that becomes vision, and with hard work and perseverance, reality. Hope is the dream of a waking man, Aristotle said, and we finished writing this book filled with hope and dreams, realizing that the more we dream, the more opportunities we have to learn from life's experience.

We shared with you all we have learned. We walk with you every stretch of the road we travel during the long time it took to write this book. We made you part of each question and each discovery. It remains to put it into practice in the areas (educational, communitarian, social settings, family) in which each one carries out his or her life. Let's walk along our journey, knowing that we are together and that the number of those who believe that one voice, added to other voices, produces the best of harmonies, when they are played in unison, is growing increasingly.

Speaking of dreams, the story of an experience

This story we are about to share is a milestone in a process that has taken years—years of drawing near, of generating trust, of advances and retreats, of mutual affection, of wanting to believe, of encouraging one another. As any encounter in life, this relationship has gone through multiple stages.

It started at the XIV Peace Conference organized by the Focolare Movement in Mariapolis Lia, in August 2010. Many occasions for dialogue and witness, both of Jews and Christians, have taken place during this conference over the past years: moments of reflection, such as in the sessions where different topics were presented, as well as in the informal moments such as at meals, musical entertainments and walks. These moments made of this conference a small laboratory of hope in our shared journey.

Moreover, we have also been involved since 2005 in the symposia of Jewish-Christian dialogue organized by the Center for Interreligious Dialogue of the Focolare Movement in Rome. We participated at two symposia in Rome, one in Jerusalem and one in Argentina. In them, and with the presence of well-known personalities at an international level, we have learned and deepened our knowledge of the contents, beliefs and emotions of both religions.

These parallel journeys have borne crucial fruits. And we say "parallel" because the methodology of the peace conferences and the symposia is the same: the Jews speak from the Jewish perspective and the Christians from their own. This has been very protecting, because it was necessary to walk on safe ground, each one with his or her own vision, walking "next" to the others, without judging or challenging them. In any event, this particular Peace Conference inspired us towards a new path. When we were asked to present a topic together, we both thought the same thing: What if instead of an individual presentation by each one, we have the courage to dialogue in front of everyone? Why don't we ask ourselves three questions that we never had the courage to formulate before, and we answer them in public?

Immediately, we experienced both joy and fear. Joy because we felt that we were growing in this experience; we trusted each other so much that we were not afraid of being questioned by the other. On the other hand, we also experienced a bit of the trepidation one has in front of the unknown, the concern of being probed by people who are not from our own tradition. Moreover, how could we ask what we wanted without hurting the other, without being aggressive or disrespectful? The questions we never had the courage to ask have to do with those gray areas that are seldom explored for fear of harming our growing experience of fraternity.

We understood that in order to keep talking about dialogue, we had to show the dialogue among us, and in this way, along with the contents of both traditions, we would be, somehow, offering tools to carry out this ideal.

Finally, the idea motivated us and challenged us to a new ground which we were in a good position to explore.

Just by being open to the challenge, we started to understand that the questions of each one aimed at very different goals. Right there, the true adventure of the spirit started, by dialoguing and by responding to the other and to ourselves.

After a few days the subjects were defined. They were not just any topics, for the gallery, but questions that would enable us to have a profound reflection on our identity and our commitment to a close relationship between Jews and Christians. They had to be sincere, respectful questions that would help us give answers comprehensible to everyone.

When we started to prepare the questions separately, we realized that the bond of trust that grew stronger between us over the years was vital; otherwise, it would have been almost impossible to deal with what we had set out to do. It would not result in a novel experience unless we appeared completely trusting of each other. The bond of trust would allow us to be incisive in our questioning, so as to bring out what was best in each other and in our religious experience. Respect for our sensibilities would lead us to use appropriate language, as clear and honest as possible, with the consciousness that the way we say things is as important as their content.

When we finally got the questions together, we realized we had not spared anything. Although they were only three questions from each, we had made it to challenge the other in core things that make the experience of dialogue between Jews and Christians substantial. Trust and affection had truly dispelled the fear of being inadequate or hurtful.

Here are the three questions that Silvina asked Francisco:

> "When we talk about God, is it really the same for both of us? Do we really, really, believe that the God, who for Judaism is abstract and omniscient, is the one who is the father of Jesus? Could it be that the name God is an ideal that for each religion refers to and means something else?"

The second was quite provocative:

> "What does it mean, really, to be the 'elder brothers'? If we are brothers, why are we so different? If we are brothers, why are there so many anti-Semites who declare themselves Christians? If we are brothers, why two thousand years of slaughter and persecution? Do we Jews like to be elder brothers? Do Christians like that we are the elder brothers, and as a result, they are the younger ones?"

And the third was not far behind:

> "What benefits will dialogue with a scattered Jewish minority bring to a major religious tradition such as Christianity?"

Francisco's questions to Silvina were of a similar scope. The first was:

> "When we interact with the Jewish community, we see many forms of being Jewish, many life-styles, many convictions (some religious, some not). Do you think a dialogue with 'Judaism' is possible? Or would we have to speak of a dialogue with 'the Jews,' or with 'every Jew'? How would you guide us Christians in order to appreciate properly (in its right dimension) unity and diversity within Judaism?"

The second and third questions referred more directly to the Judeo-Christian dialogue:

> "What can encourage Jews to strive to reach out and to understand Christians? In your opinion, can the relationship with Christians contribute anything to the understanding that Jews have of themselves and of the world?"

> "From your personal perspective, at what stage of maturity is the dialogue between Jews and Christians? What are the next steps into the future? What are the long-term goals to achieve?"

It was not easy to face these questions and answer them, bearing in mind not only what our faith and tradition say, but also the speakers and all the participants of the Peace Conference.[1] This was a unique opportunity to put into practice the two loyalties we spoke about in the first chapter, and to implement a mode and a method to express our experience.

These six questions were the trigger of an extraordinary experience. Each of us prepared the responses separately and we met the day of the conference to compare them.

As a first step of mutual care, we decided to review the answers which each one had prepared in order to avoid surprises in public. It was sort of an "insurance" against potential accidents that could damage ourselves and hurt the others.

Thus we read the answers together in private, asking for clarifications, and inquiring about the meaning we gave to certain words or expressions, which are common code for one side, while having other connotations for the other.

We would like to mention a few examples:

1. The Peace Conferences have been held since 1996 in Mariapolis Lia, O'Higgins, Buenos Aires. They bring together Christians and Jews in fellowship for an exchange of ideas, traditions and beliefs in order to promote peace and dialogue.

Francisco read the answer regarding the Triune God of Christians and said: "The One and Only God of Israel is also for Christians the One and Only God. However, within his intimacy, God is communion, a mutual gift of self among distinct persons. God is One and is multiple, God is One and Triune." To which Silvina, perplexed, replied: "That is a tongue-twister."

Beyond the humor of the story, it is interesting to understand what was happening. Francisco was familiar with the expressions, but the same words were unintelligible for Silvina. We think we speak the same language and sometimes we don't take the time to confirm whether the other understands the meaning of what we are saying. That changed the presentation of Francisco before the audience, so that everyone could understand.

In another place Francisco wrote referring to Israel as the "chosen people." The expression, "chosen people," which affirms the special relationship of God with Israel and, as a consequence, with the Christian people, connoted for Silvina something that had historically caused a great deal of pain, with negative consequences for the relationship between Jews and Christians. Many times the hatred and the persecution of Jews was based on the supposed Jewish privilege of having been chosen by God, almost at the expense of other peoples. Therefore, Silvina asked Francisco not to use that expression in that way. For her, the concept of the people elected by God had to be deepened before expressing it as something natural. This did not mean to relativize the meaning of a concept that is fundamental for many; but we can't ignore that the same words can have different connotations. That's why this journey compels us to make an effort to explain controversial expressions so that all may have access to the same meaning. What creates strong feelings should not be omitted, but neither should it be imposed; we must learn to sort it out until we understand its true dimensions.

On the other hand, the assertion of Silvina regarding Judaism as a religion was very enlightening for Francisco: "As a first approach, it is essential to clarify that Judaism is not a religion." This may sound paradoxical to Christian ears. Are we not engaging in dialogue between religions? This is why it was so significant to understand that the concept of religion for the Christian world is different from what it signifies for the Jewish world, where the concept of people, culture and tradition prevails, in which religiosity is just one of its aspects. As we see again, the same words acquire different meanings, which stem from texts and history. Thus we have an obligation to explain, even if the difference is minimal, because otherwise a small disagreement can lead to a big separation.

It was an amazing experience because we did notice, once more, the need to grasp in depth what we are saying when we affirm or deny something, when we use one word or another, when we express an idea that for us is "normal" and that for the other can be confusing, incomprehensible or even hurtful.

As a result, we delved into this work of genuine, mutual understanding very seriously. I think we, ourselves, were the first to be benefitted by the effort. It was a construction together, truly together, which did not deny the respective identities and the natural diversity among us. This would have been impossible, we repeat, had not there been a bond of trust and understanding between us and a suitable environment, such as the Day of Peace, which has years of tradition and a constant search for brotherhood between Jews and Christians.

Finally, with our responses, weighed together, we arrived at the afternoon panel. Everyone understood that it was not a debate where one tries to convince the other of his or her position; not even a match between two people who want to make themselves understood at all cost.

Each of us read the question made by the other and answered it. Mutual listening, which we had experienced in the preparation of the panel, was transmitted to the audience. The participants of the Day welcomed the questions and answers with unusual attention and interest, which surprised everyone present, including ourselves. It was an experience that went beyond our expectations and that signified a contribution to the growth in this journey of dialogue we have taken.

The questions and the answers

The questions were the engine for two types of content: relational and informational. The questions had two dimensions: one gave clues as to how to enter into the other; the second clarified our position before each question.

Here we transcribe the questions Silvina asked Francisco as well as his answers:

1) When we talk about God, is it really the same for both of us? Do we really, really, believe that the God, who for Judaism is abstract and omniscient, is the one who is the father of Jesus? Could it be that the name God is an ideal that for each religion refers to and means something else?

A somehow superficial answer would be to say that actually Jews and Christians do not speak about the same God.

The One and Only God of Israel is, for Christians too, the One and Only God. However, within His intimacy, God is communion, is constant and mutual gift of self between distinct persons: The Father, the Son and the Holy Spirit. All three are God and each one is God. God, in the Christian experience, is One and Three. Thanks to that mutual gift of self, the Father is Father because He generates the Son out of love. The Son is such because he responds to the Father with the same love that he received. The Love flowing between both of them, the "atmosphere" in which Father and Son live, is a person: the Holy Spirit.

It's a real "mystery" of the Christian faith: among the mystics and Christian thinkers the assertion is well known that when we grasp something about the Triune God, the image that appears to us is that God is One; when we make it to understand better that God is One, his being Triune grabs our attention. We see God as someone "articulated," where each of the divine persons is present in the other, each one is God, but God is the communion of the Three. And God is One.

In short, we are before a mystery of love, because love makes us be "one" (of the same family, of the same community, identifying with the other in their grief or joy); at the same time, love makes us be ourselves. Love involves a gift of self and a communion, the sense of family and unity. Simultaneously, there is respect for the other, for the other's different personality, for the identity that makes the others be who they are, and that makes me be who I am.

The apostle John, in his first letter[2] says that God is Love.[3] This statement, and the experience of Jesus and the Church in its early centuries, have helped Christians approach the mystery of God. We face a paradox, between the absolutely Simple and the absolutely Complex, the fundamental Richness and the fundamental Simplicity.

God, for Christians, is not only the father of Jesus: God is Father, is Son and the Spirit of Love that flows between both: the Holy Spirit.

What seem to be almost a tongue-twister has large consequences in practical life: what does it mean for the lives of Christians to live like the Triune God? How is unity and diversity lived within a community? What implications does Trinitarian faith have in the relationship of Christians with other religions, with the world?

---

2. Three letters to nascent Christian communities are attributed to the apostle John, which are part of what we know as the Second Testament.
3. 1 John 4:8.

Now, you could say to me, "You were right, we're not talking about the same God that we Jews know." I think this may be the fundamental point of our encounter and also of our disagreement.

Christians believe that the God who accompanied Israel in its history, who cared for it, nurtured it and spoke to it, is the same God who accompanied Jesus in his life, nurtured him, and spoke through his words. When we read the Gospel, we say at the end: "This is the Word of God." It's not surprising that this sounds rather strong for Jews.

It should be noted that what I have said thus far stems from the Christian perspective. That is, there are not two gods, one for Christians and another for Jews. God is One and Only. We have different experiences of Him. If this is so, why? God is mysterious—we can't grasp him, put him in our heads and our language—and although He made himself known to Israel, for Christians He is the God of all people. We can look for him on the road that He himself planned for us and made us travel on, as individuals and as communities.

To the extent that we get closer to Him, we are, somehow also in a mysterious way, closer among us. The main challenge of our dialogue is to delve into the experience of God offered and lived by the other's tradition.

2) What does it mean, really, to be the 'elder brothers'? If we are brothers, why are we so different? If we are brothers, why are there so many anti-Semites who declare themselves Christians? If we are brothers, why two thousand years of slaughter and persecution? Do we Jews like to be elder brothers? Do Christians like that we are the elder brothers, and as a result, they are the younger ones?

I would like to quote the exact phrases that John Paul II pronounced in the synagogue in Rome, when he spoke of the Jews as our elder brothers. The Pope said:

The Jewish religion is not "extrinsic" to us, but in a certain way it is "intrinsic" to our own religion. With

Judaism therefore we have a relationship which we do not have with any other religion. You are our dearly beloved brothers and, in a certain way, it could be said that you are our elder brothers.

The words *"in a certain way,"* caught my attention. The Pope affirms that Jews are our "beloved" brothers, but he doesn't state categorically that they are our elder brothers.

It is not difficult for Christians to consider the Jews as "their elder brothers." We feel we are children of Abraham, we have in common the same scriptures, we believe in the God who spoke to Israel and held a covenant with his people.

Like many siblings, we fought about issues regarding the paternal inheritance with catastrophic consequences: one of the siblings became powerful and the other was dispersed and persecuted.

Brothers exist by birth, it is inevitable. But we recognize each other as brothers only if we treat each other as such. It took two thousand years for Jews and Christians to learn fraternity and recognize each other as brothers. Why? We would need to refer not only to theology, which evidently divides us, but also to sociology and psychology, in order to explain why a sibling has the need to annul the other in order to feel that he is the son of his father.

Let's address the questions: Do we Jews like to be elder brothers? Do Christians like that we are the elder brothers, and as a result, they are the younger ones?

I think the Church and her main representatives have grown mature enough to recognize it. I am referring to John Paul II, but also to the document *Nostra Aetate* and subsequent documents referring to the relationship between Jews and Christians. It follows then that the Church, in her magisterium and teaching, feels comfortable with this expression and is fully aware that Christians and Jews are brothers, distinct—of course—but brothers in the end.

There are clearly anti-Semitic people who are baptized and define themselves as Christians. This is a great contradiction within the Church that we have to fight against and we are committed to do so.

Finally, I wonder whether we are brothers who are "so" different, especially if we consider other human beings, with whom we also need to build bonds of fraternity, and have few common cultural and religious parameters. In reality, we are different, but we have many things in common, as usually happens between siblings who still have a long way to go in building fraternity.

With regards to whether Jews feel comfortable with the expression "elder brothers," we would need to ask you.

3) What benefits will dialogue with a scattered Jewish minority bring to a major religious tradition such as Christianity?

I cannot account for all the motivations that Christians who engage in dialogue have. I don't know them fully and I could not mention them exactly. However, I can say that for the church community, the dialogue with Judaism implies the progressive recognition of the brotherhood that unites us, and this gives us the possibility of sharing—each in its own way—the paternal home. The joint witness of Jews and Christians is vital to the relationship with the rest of humanity. It involves a combined effort to collaborate in a practical way in many issues regarding justice and the social order. We share the experience of the Revelation that God wanted to make to mankind through Israel. Knowing each other and living together helps both of us to deepen our own religious experience and, in turn, to increase our ability to open up to the other and to others.

Dialogue implies mutual knowledge, intellectual recognition of what we have in common, and radical respect for differences.

For Christians, knowledge of and dialogue with Jews help to eradicate, where it still remains, the irrationality of anti-Semitism. It's not good for any person or community to allow in itself evil seeds that may grow, develop and lead to the destruction of others, and consequently, of oneself. "I cannot hurt you without hurting myself."

Now, the questions of Francisco to Silvina, and her answers.

1) When we interact with the Jewish community, we see many forms of being Jewish, many life-styles, many convictions (some religious, some not). Do you think a dialogue with 'Judaism' is possible? Or would we have to speak of a dialogue with 'the Jews,' or with 'every Jew'? How would you guide us Christians in order to appreciate properly (in its right dimension) unity and diversity within Judaism?

First, we should clarify that Judaism is not based on a universal vision, valid for everyone—what is called a dogmatic body,— but it has at its core the vision of an interpretive tradition in constant renewal. Such interpretations are not necessarily validated by any institution. Thus, my answers to questions of this kind are the product of my personal position, agreed upon by many, and the result of years of reading and debate. But they don't constitute an official position because, in fact, it does not exist as such.

The millennia old and complex Jewish people have an almost unique characteristic at a demographic level: their culture, legal corpus and beliefs have unfurled while being dispersed throughout the world, exiled from their homeland, and in contact with different civilizations and ways of thinking. This has developed what the Israeli-American rabbi, philosopher and educator, David Hartman, defined as an "interpretive tradition."

Throughout the history of the Jewish people, there were always several, often conflicting, interpretive currents. What it is important for our tradition is not so much the search for a unique truth, but the study of the living text, in order to dialogue with it and allow the necessary interpretations, so that each generation may learn from it and possess its valuable wisdom, in each historical and social period.

As a first approach, it is essential to clarify that Judaism is not a religion, per se, although it has been necessary to frame it in this category in order to accept that Jews could be French or Italian, without having to renounce their Judaism. However, belonging to the Jewish people does not imply a monolithic membership linked exclusively to rituals and beliefs. It is an affiliation to a genealogical tree, a culture, an ethical paradigm, a calendar with commemorations and celebrations, a common time, a messianic hope, a dream of returning to live all in the same land, etc. Can one be legitimately Jewish and legitimately Argentine? This is a frequent question with a very easy answer: there is no contradiction in both affiliations.

The evolution of human beings and societies also produced, in its conversation with Judaism, different movements of adaptation to the realities and paradigms of each time. Hence you may have heard of Orthodox, Reform and Conservative Jews, even of secular and humanist Jews. We all have the same text but each interprets it in different ways.

So, I think sometimes dialogue becomes difficult from the very beginning. Why? Because you may not understand who you are talking to, who is the speaker on the side of Judaism, and who does he or she represent within the Jewish map. The first challenge lies in this difficulty.

2) What can encourage Jews to strive to reach out and to understand Christians? In your opinion, can the relationship with Christians contribute anything to the understanding that Jews have of themselves and of the world?

I could not claim, without arrogance, to know what can motivate Jews to dialogue with Christians. I can say what motivates *me* to participate in experiences of dialogue and interfaith activities. I know that two thousand years of suffering will not heal with just a few attempts; however, I feel the strong desire to know today's Christians in order to listen to their positions with regards to history and the future; but, above all, I need them to listen to me, perhaps to give a voice to those Jewish brothers who were silenced because of who they were.

I have made the decision to throw myself into it and make myself known, because you can only love what you know. I do not pretend to be loved personally, but as part of the Jewish people, I aspire to be known to avoid being isolated or feared, and to banish stereotypes that come from ignorance or unexamined repetition. I do it because in this journey I meet good people, people who take their chances to build a better world. Moreover, when I run into someone who attacks or questions me, I see then an opportunity to strengthen my answers, to assess my ability to reach out, explain, be patient and respectful of the others and of myself. But fundamentally, I do it to leave my children a possible pathway of hope, as well as the tools to support the pride in their identity, including diversity, as part of the miracle of all that is human. In my view, the relationship with Christians and with any others, contributes richness, questioning and searches for empathy and meaning.

3) From your personal perspective, at what stage of maturity is the dialogue between Jews and Christians? What are the next steps into the future? What are the long-term goals to achieve?

Much has been done and many roads have been travelled; however, if I think about at what stage the dialogue is, I'd venture to say that it has only just begun. We are in a time of shared monologues, where respect and the desire to know the other take precedence. Steps toward the future will be defined as we journey together, as we stumble and recover. There is no other choice but to keep on trying, one by one, step by step, because dialogue cannot be decreed or imposed, but it will come from people's willingness to get to know each other in "useless" ways—if I may say so—in a time so materialistic and sensationalist. It will come from the desire to spend time in activities with no immediate returns. I think the keys are education, in general, and the mutual contact and acquaintance of children and young people, in particular, before prejudices are not entirely settled in them.

By way of conclusion

The most interesting part of the whole experience was what happened to the audience. First, there were several participants who vigorously waved their hands to ask to speak in order to answer the "other." For example, when Silvina was listening to Francisco's response on the Triune God, a member of the Jewish community wanted to "respond" to Francisco in order to explain the concept of the divine in Judaism. It was an illustrative moment: we immediately intervened and explained that the basis for dialogue, especially in religious matters, is to know how to respect the question of one and the other's response, without "retorting" from one's own position. In this case, the objective was to understand the concept of divinity in the Christian tradition. There was no reason to speak about the Jewish concept of God, since Francisco had not asked about it.

This enables an unbiased listening, it entails making room for the other without having to compete or invade. Dialogue means to be interested in the other, without implying that one loses prominence. At times, keeping quiet, attentive to the words of the other, trying to understand them fully, will transform us much more into main players than if we were to always display a state of contention, of alarm, because the other represents a certain danger. When we appear in a permanent state of confrontation we become weak, even if we imagine that this is the way to show our strength. Confrontations are not always violent. Many times, in the name of cordiality, we can commit acts that harm the integrity of the others. But when we appear humble, open, and curious about the other, without wanting to win the battle—because we have understood that we are not in any battle—then, we all win.

The truth is that the general atmosphere—the meeting room was filled with adults and many young people—was one of absolute silence. We could characterize it as a profound emotional silence, an illuminating attention, a certain sense of joy to be witnessing a real experience of communion.

After our presentation, many young people came to thank us; one could see the sparkle of hope in their eyes. Someone remarked: "I just saw in person what we have always been taught and that I thought to be rather utopian." A young Jew told us: "I think this would have been impossible years ago. We have taken a very important step."

Several times we repeated that what we said to each other—which was deep and often quite strong,—we could do it only because of the trust, the respectful listening, the careful wording and the affection that we have for one another. You could say that one could "see" our mutual affection; this comforts any audience and, even more so, ourselves.

The long applause of the participants was touching. And we too were touched. Because the experience also surprised us. And that's the beauty of this journey through the intricacies of the human soul: never stop pondering the fact that there are always opportunities for growth, that no one has the last word, and that despite the darkness, it is never in vain to persevere in order to find a ray of light that can show us the way.

Afterwards, we heard many opinions and comments from some of the participants. One of the phrases we remember most is that of a woman who said: "But this is useful not only for interreligious dialogue, but also for all other dialogues, in our homes, in our jobs. How many times we pretend we are listening, while all we are doing is preparing our own response."

In short, we were experiencing a great discovery. We had grown in the dialogue and we had a lot to learn from this experience. We had to process many new concepts in order to elaborate theoretically what had been born out of a genuine intuition and many years of development.

Afterword

Ten Principles for Dialogue

MARTIN BUBER TELLS A story, from the time he was a university counselor, about a young student who confessed to him his personal drama. Busy with other matters, Dr. Buber didn't give much importance to their conversation. The next day he read in the university newspaper that this student had committed suicide. He was so shocked that it led him to further develop his theory of, what came to be called, dialogic philosophy, a philosophy of dialogue.

The dialogic philosophy stems from the idea that there are two relational terms, the "I-Thou" and the "I-It." When we speak of "I" we never refer to the "I" in its individual dimension, because there is no single dimension of self. When we refer to the "I" it is always done in function of the "Thou " or the "It." So Buber's premise is that the "I" in the "I-Thou" relationship differs from the "I" in the "I-It" relationship.

When we speak of the "I-It," we refer to the relationship that a person establishes with a third person or with an object, perceiving the other person as an object. Instead, the "I-Thou" relationship is established so that I can perceive and treat people or objects as if they were people.

This implies that the relationship with third persons can at times be more fluid, and the relationship with those who are closer to us may be more distant.

171

Martin Buber concludes then that dialogue is the profound sharing of human existence that results in co-existence.

When we speak of dialogue in any sense, we are referring to the possibility of an "I-Thou" relationship. Therefore, dialogue can exist only among men, among human beings. There is no dialogue between organizations, between institutions, between countries or continents.

Under this conceptual framework:

1. We should examine whether there is dialogue between East and West. It may seem a truism, but it isn't, because dialogue between countries, organizations, and cultures is nothing but dialogue between people. If there is not a dialogic attitude among men, it will be impossible to have dialogue between organizations. If institutional dialogue existed, world peace would be resolved by the United Nations. The problem is the lack of dialogue between men. This has to do with a second point.

2. There is no dialogue without a common language, which implies a language of values. According to Noam Chomsky, it's all a matter of linguistics. When we say "language," we are talking about values. At this point we should return to the old manual *Introduction to Logic* by Irving Copi, who insists that in order to understand the other's language, we need "to stick to the common use." I think that returning to the common usage of the language of words in function of the language of values is a very big help for understanding the East and the West, to understand one and the other, to understand the dialogic sense of " I-Thou."

3. Some values are comparable; some are incomparable and some are incompatible. If we don't understand this range in the role of the language and of the value, we are not grasping exactly what the concept of value represents. Dialogue means working

on common usage. Are we talking about the same thing when we talk about the same thing?

I always remember that my father suffered from heartburn, and once I asked him: What is heartburn? He said: "It is something that comes to you from inside here." Up to now, I'm not sure whether when I have heartburn is the same heartburn that my father had. Translating the compatibility of sensations into words is one of the elements that can help to understand the meaning of value.

I give another example which has to do with this topic and that will eventually lead to a third one. The Israeli satirist Ephraim Kishon had invented a character coming from Yemen, who was arriving in Israel. This is a world of different cultures and trying to put together and make cultures equivalent is quite a difficult task. He tells the story of a meeting that occurs between the Yemeni and a member of a kibbutz, a collective village. The latter was from Germany, with all its development of socialist values and a superior "culture" (I say this with irony). On the other hand, when Yemenis were moved to Israel, they went to live, at the beginning, in very precarious conditions, in quite miserable housing. So the German says to him, "we are living in the twentieth century," and the Yemeni responds: "no, we are living in the slums." The German will then say, "the twentieth century is not a place to live" and the Yemeni tells him, "neither are the slums." Beyond the irony, in dialogue it is necessary to understand the categories of space and time as distinct categories. The concept of space and time is not the same for everyone. The concept of time may not be the same when we speak of "sacred time" and "profane time." There are sacred times and profane times, and there are sacred places and profane places. To respect dialogue means to understand the times and the spaces of the other, within the times and the spaces of oneself.

4. Another example: I recently visited Morocco. Our tourist guide was a Muslim, a very pleasant man. During the outing, he had sort of an argument with a lady of the group who was from Cordoba. She jokingly said, "you're a liar." And the guide replied, "At most you can say that you don't agree with me, but my tradition forbids me to lie." What for one was a joke, to the other could become an offense. Here I want to emphasize the role of language, and the topic of truth and falsehood. How to deal with the differences? It must be logically understood that there are many sides of the truth that can't be seen completely. Truths are opportunities in which the other can be a partner in the search. William Sloane Coffin, a leading Protestant theologian, used to say, "I believe in seekers of truth, not in possessors of truth."

Inasmuch as we are anchored in our "truths," we will not be able to appreciate that there are other truths that we do not understand. In this, it is very important the aid of science in front of the space of religion and beliefs.

5. The indispensable dialogue is the "dialogic" dialogue, which is the opposite of "platonic" dialogue, whose quest is to convince the other.

While the Platonic dialogue comes "with-win" ("convince," in Latin), the "dialogical dialogue" is the one that comes "without–win," without the intent to defeat the other, that is, without leaving different from the way one entered. If we are not willing to have the experience of dialogue, then, we haven't understood exactly what dialogue is. In the dialogue "with-win", we think that we have the truth and the power of reason, and the only thing we try is to impose them.

Dialogue without winning requires, without economic, political, cultural and religious reductionisms, listening, love, understanding and transformation.

6. We need to break away from dualism, while understanding distinctions. But we can't start from the basis that there is reason and spirit, spirit and matter,

politics and religion, religion and State, private and public. Breaking away from dualism means to start with a similar premise, by walking, going, accompanying, in the same dimension.

7. We must understand the meaning of progress in an existential way. Progress is not quality of life and improvement of the quantitative (the material). Progress denotes the level of respect in the development of pluralism, as well as understanding that plural societies are those in which plural persons, in their individuality and subjectivity, dialogue; they are people who are willing to dialogue.

8. To be aware that the ten commandments are not universal; they belong to a certain world, but not to all the diverse worlds that exist in the universe.

9. When we speak of a "clash of civilizations" and "overcoming fundamentalisms," we imply overcoming our own fundamentalisms, calling into question our own foundations as a mental exercise, in order to understand the foundations of the other. And here I rule out the word "tolerance" from the social language. Because tolerance is always exercised from a position of power; and it suggests that I endure because I have the superiority of being able to endure. But in reality "tolerance" or "political tolerance" is nothing other than showing the guarantee that I have to justify my own fundamentalism.

10. We must help overcome the traumas of history, aware that progress is made with memory and justice, not with oblivion or amnesia.

Therefore, the invitation to a "dialogue among civilizations" means a "dialogue between men"; to be prepared to understand the language of the other in its moral category; to be open enough to understand that there are different logics, different reasons, different spirits, with no other intention than understanding me.

Insofar as I understand and realize that the other wants to understand me, we'll be waiting with hope for a future that can be different from the past that we've built up to the present.

Rabbi Daniel Goldman
Community Beth El (Buenos Aires, Argentina)

Educating for Dialogue

In the current landscape of our Argentinean society, being in contact with people of different cultures and religions is alive and unavoidable. It is a providential opportunity to experience that the true religious sense can promote authentic relationships of universal brotherhood. Today, living and witnessing the faith with sincere and respectful love favors an openness to dialogue which does not imply imposing or renouncing one's own identity. This requires a dedication to others that comes from the heart, and that recognizes the wealth of humanity that each person and community possess.

In this dynamic of relationships, both word and silence come into play: two moments that alternate and are integrated into a communication of value and meaning. In our fast-paced and deafening world, silence regains its special value. Without silence, words lose density and content; we don't understand what we mean or what we expect of the other.

We allow the one before us to speak and express himself by our being silent, as opposed to being closed in ourselves or clinging to our words or ideas. Mutual listening opens a fuller space of human relationship. It is the right environment, made of words, exchanges and reflections, to welcome the deeper questions. Silence is more eloquent than a hurried answer because it doesn't speed up the time or spare us the maturity of the journey.

Learning how to communicate and to educate for dialogue helps us to listen, to contemplate, besides speaking, and thus to distinguish what is important from what is useless or superficial. A sincere and mutual dialogue helps us discover the existing relationship between

177

situations that at first sight seem disconnected, to value and analyze their messages; to share opinions and convictions; and it causes a genuine, shared knowledge. This challenges us to create together an environment that balances silence and words, images and sounds.

It is perhaps attained only by a heart that loves and accepts the others with their originality and richness. "Love is the light—and in the end, the only light—that can always illuminate a world grown dim and give us the courage needed to keep living and working." (DCE 39). In this way, "the Christian's program—the program of the Good Samaritan, the program of Jesus—is 'a heart which sees.' This heart sees where love is needed and acts accordingly." (cf. DCE 31).

Most Reverend Ramón Alfredo Dus
Archibishop of Resistencia, Chaco, Argentina

New City Press of the Focolare

New City Press is one of more than 20 publishing houses sponsored by the Focolare, a movement founded by Chiara Lubich to help bring about the realization of Jesus' prayer: "That all may be one" (John 17:21). In view of that goal, New City Press publishes books and resources that enrich the lives of people and help all to strive toward the unity of the entire human family. We are a member of the Association of Catholic Publishers.

202 Comforter Blvd., Hyde Park, NY 12538
www.newcitypress.com

The Jewish Theological Seminary

The Jewish Theological Seminary (JTS) is a preeminent institution of Jewish higher education that integrates rigorous academic scholarship and teaching with a commitment to strengthening Jewish tradition, Jewish lives, and Jewish communities. The Milstein Center for Interreligious Dialogue at JTS is its arm for interreligious programming and engagement through public events, consultations, and publications.

3080 Broadway, New York, NY 10027
www.jtsa.edu

Further Reading

Walking Together, Jews and Christians in Dialogue
978-88-6739-022-9 $19.95

Un dialogo para la vida   978-950-586-298-6 $22.00

Muslims Ask, Christians Answer   978-1-56548-430-6 $15.95

Living Dialogue   978-1-56548-326-2 $9.95

5 Steps to Living Christian Unity   978-1-56548-501-3 $4.95

Scan to join our mailing list for discounts and promotions
or go to
www.newcitypress.com
and click on "join our email list."